Light on Adoption

Rabekah Scott-Heart

First published in 2022 by Rabekah Scott-Heart
Brisbane, Australia

© 2022 Rabekah Scott-Heart
W: facebook.com/ShiningLightOnAdoption

All rights reserved. Except as permitted under the Australian Copyright Act 1968, no part of this publication may be reproduced, stored in a retrieval system, or transmitted in any form or by any means, electronic, mechanical, photocopying, recording or otherwise, without prior written permission from the publisher. All enquiries should be made to the author.

Author: Rabekah Scott-Heart
Title: Light on Adoption
E-book ISBN: 9780645527315
Paperback ISBN: 9780645527322
Subjects: Adoption | Family Relationships
Registered with the National Library of Australia
Book production services: www.smartwomenpublish.com

 A catalogue record for this book is available from the National Library of Australia

Disclaimer:
The material in this publication is of the nature of general comment only and does not represent professional advice. All material is provided for educational purposes only. We recommend to always seek the advice of a qualified professional before making any decision regarding personal and business needs. To the maximum extent permitted by law, the author and publisher disclaim all responsibility and liability to any person arising directly or indirectly from any person taking or not taking action based on the information in this publication.

In loving memory

With a deep sense of loss, love and gratitude,

I dedicate this book to my beloved soul mate, Joe Scott.

Joe imparted the great gifts of passion

and purpose to all who knew him.

He lived his life fully with joy and enthusiasm.

And his love of flying lives on through

the many people who were taken under his wing.

Contents

Preface 7
Introduction 15

1	Mamatoto	19
2	Building a House on Sand	27
3	Odyssey	33
4	Ireland	41
5	Mental Health	47
6	Rejection	59
7	Invisibility	67
8	Grief	73
9	Disenfranchised Grief	79
10	Misfits and Fringe Dwellers	89
11	Implicit and Explicit Memory	99
12	Meeting My Mother	103
13	Inner Reunion	113
14	Inner Child	123
15	Reclaiming Your Inner Child	127
16	My Devastating Wake-up Call	133
17	Love Your Self	145
18	Bold Is Beautiful	151
19	Know Your Vulnerabilities and Triggers	157
20	Forgiven Not Forgotten	165

21	Home to the Heart	169
22	Changing the Script	173
23	Alchemy	199
24	Uncomfortable Truths	203
25	Magic Carpet Ride	211
26	Return	215
27	Community	221

Preface

'Oh! why does the wind blow upon me so wild?
Is it because I am nobody's child?'

—Phila H Case, 'Nobody's Child'

When I met my birth mother at the age of twenty-nine, she told me, 'I'm sorry, you don't feel like a part of me.' I knew I wasn't a part of my adoptive mother either when she said, 'I wonder what my own daughter would have been like.'

I don't blame either of my mothers for their insensitivity, but I do hold accountable a callous adoption system that has broken the bonds, hearts and lives of many thousands of people within my adoption community.

As I sit and write on the wild and windy Isle of Skye in Scotland, I think back to my defiant days, when I rebelled and fought in anger. I fought against authority, against the men in my life, and against the rules. Beneath my fierce rebellion and explosive rage was a lot of hurt and pain. I felt less than, disconnected, insubstantial and unlovable.

I am one of millions of adoptees around the world who were amputated from their mothers at birth. That seismic event irrevocably changed the course of my life.

I am an amputee; I was severed from my mother at birth.

I am an adoptee; my right to grieve, and my sense of safety, trust, security, belonging, and identity were stolen from me.

I am an adaptee; my body and mind have had to construct ways to adapt, to cope with catastrophic trauma.

Imagine cutting off a person's arm and leaving them to bleed. Maybe you wrap them up in a blanket, set them down on a bed and let them scream. Or you give them a sedative to shut them up. This painful analogy describes what has been done to adoptees, whose wounds, although invisible, are no less grievous.

Mother and baby are one connected entity. It's impossible to quantify the damage caused by amputating a newborn from their mother. We wouldn't take a puppy or kitten away from their mother at birth, and yet the adoption system had no reservations about depriving human babies of the developmental needs and nourishment necessary for a healthy start to life.

There were approximately 250,000 forced adoptions in Australia between 1950 and 1975. I was born in 1961, when adoptable babies were precious commodities in high demand.

I was adopted by a kind, broken-hearted and emotionally distant English woman, and my adoptive father was a sadistic, narcissistic

Scottish-Irish man. The gone-to-a-good home propaganda didn't apply to my dysfunctional adoptive family, or many others.

For much of my life I didn't know that birth trauma and adoption were at cause of my problems with depression and anxiety. In her book, *The Primal Wound*, Nancy Verrier writes that the unavailability of conscious recall of individuals who were separated from their mothers at birth has contributed to many misconceptions about relinquishment and adoption.

The wounds of adoption can lie deeply hidden and undetected by adoptees themselves, and by many health professionals who don't realise that relinquishment trauma is a primary issue, but rather treat the emanating symptoms. Depression, anxiety, addiction, and struggles in relationships are some of the consequences of the critical-attachment injury that adoptees sustained at birth.

Removing newborns from their mothers is a magnitude-ten earthquake upon their foundation. It has been my lifelong occupation to dig through the rubble, beneath the layers of artifice and coping strategies, to ultimately unearth my essential self. Thankfully, our true selves are never destroyed. And paradoxically, in the words of Katherine Mackenett, 'Mountains don't rise without earthquakes.' May all adoptees rise masterful and resilient in the wake of their personal devastation.

In *Light on Adoption*, I reveal some of the complex consequences of separation trauma, adoption loss and grief, and I hope that this awareness will lead to more sensitivity and support for the natural-birth process. Taking a baby from their mother at birth—from their clan and identity—severs that child's roots completely. Just as an uprooted plant needs special care and conditions if it is to be successfully transplanted and take root in its new environment, so too does a human being. Every living thing needs the right kind of nurturing to thrive, or it will be a withered version of its healthy potential. As the twig is bent, so grows the tree.

Like many adoptees, my own transplant didn't go well. I suffered a very anxious and unhappy childhood, and beyond. I felt like a hollow ghost. I wasn't anchored to my body. I didn't feel human, so I studied what humans around me did and said, and I tried very hard to fit in. Feeling like an alien is extremely isolating. I felt no bonded connection to any members of my adoptive family. My only sense of comfort and connection was with my animal friends, or when I was alone in nature.

When a child is born and immediately taken from their mother, that child's authentic self suffers an earth-shattering injury. The child loses a sense of stability, safety, and secure attachment. They are taken from the comfort and concord of their mother's womb and cast into the bleak abyss of disconnectedness. Separated babies experience both birth and death in their first moments.

Without specialised care to support adopted children to express their grief, and convalesce, and learn how to manage the effects of their trauma and loss, many adult adoptees still live with the compounding consequences of adoption. Separation trauma can manifest as a vague sense of something missing, or an undercurrent of melancholy, to more obvious and debilitating symptoms such as chronic anxiety, depression, substance abuse, and recurrent relationship problems. Or as my adopted friend once described: 'a subtle and persistent drive to feel safe and accepted', and to fit in as if her very survival depended on it.

Unlike many other sufferers of traumatic stress, adoptees have no pre-trauma reference. How can we know that we have experienced trauma at birth without explicit memory of the experience, or an environment that validated our trauma?

A returned soldier, a child who loses a parent, someone whose partner dies in an accident, all these people can reference those events and put their pain into perspective. And in most cases, they receive sympathy and support for their socially sanctioned loss and grief.

This is not the case for adoptees. Instead, we were told that we were lucky to have been chosen, and that we should be grateful. We were saved the stigma of illegitimacy and given to good homes with 'respectable married parents'. There was no recognition of our loss, pain or grief. We were effectively gaslit; our true feelings and perceptions of our reality were overridden and denied by adoption advertising. Are any other victims of trauma told they are lucky and special? Imagine a child who has suffered the catastrophic sudden loss of a parent. Now imagine that, instead of being given comfort, reassurance and support to express their grief, the child is told that they are lucky!

It has taken me sixty years to find my voice. I have had to overcome the internalised and oppressive adoption edict that any negative feelings I have regarding my adoption are a prohibited subject. I've spent much of my life playing the role of the acquiescent, diplomatic adoptee, pleasing everyone around me and complying with the notion that I should be grateful for having been adopted. I've been very good at being the good girl.

I have written *this book* to highlight some of the lesser known realities of adoption, and to expose the invisible underbelly of the happy-ever-after myth. *Light on Adoption* aims to break through the clouds of denial and ignorance that have shrouded the enduring impact of forced adoption on adoptees. Wounds need light and air to heal. Unhealed wounds worsen when left unattended, and can infect a life like a slow poison, undermining relationships, health and happiness. Birth trauma and adoption loss has caused grievous psychological, emotional and physical harm to countless adoptees in Australia and around the world. Adoptees are twice as likely to suffer from mood disorders, are over-represented in drug- and alcohol-treatment centres, and four times more likely to attempt suicide than non-adopted people. In one support group I facilitated, seven out of eleven adoptees had a history of depression, and alcohol and drug addiction, and two had attempted suicide.

Forced-adoption practices sanctioned a human-rights violation; an erasure of the most essential link a human being is entitled to: a link to their family and identity. It was a callous crime that committed thousands of mothers and their children to a lifetime sentence of unresolved grief.

What doesn't kill you makes you stronger, and I believe it's time for my adoption community to be recognised for our struggles and strengths in a new dawn of awareness, understanding and healing.

I am writing primarily to and for my fellow adoptees. I hope that *Light on Adoption* gives some clarity, solace and support to my community. Many of us have suffered the effects of separation trauma without any compassionate enquiry, understanding or validation. The reality of our experience was overlaid with messages such as: we were fortunate to have gone to a good home, and we were loved so much that we were given away.

This book has been a long labour of love. It's an articulation of my life's work, which has been to understand the impact of adoption on my psyche, my emotions, my heart and my soul. After many years of therapy, self-help, searching, tragedies, trials and errors, research, reflection and determined effort, I have recovered my self. At long last I fully inhabit my body. I finally feel settled in my skin and accept myself as I am. I am what I am. I have bonded ... to *me*.

I offer what I've learned to a society that continues to deny the sanctity of infant-mother bonding. *Light on Adoption* illuminates the challenges and the complicated tumult of thoughts and feelings that many adoptees grapple with on a daily basis. Understanding the trauma and losses inherent in the adoption process is an important step in adoptee reparation. It is possible to repair any damage done to our internal foundation, and rebuild a life beyond past wounds into an inspired future of our own design.

What I share in this book won't resonate with everyone, so please excuse me for using the convenient collective 'we' or 'adoptees', and siphon through your own filter what does and doesn't resound for you. I acknowledge that there will be exceptions to the circumstances I have described in these pages, and not every adoptee will relate to my personal story, or agree with what I've presented. I respect that everyone's version of the truth will be unique according to their individual experience.

I want to encourage more adoptees—people who understand life through the particular lens of birth trauma and adoption—to come together and support each other to talk about our individual adoption experiences. By telling our truth-full stories we can effect positive change—for ourselves, our communities, and a more compassionate society. When we rise and shine, and collectively contribute the wisdom of our lived experience, we will cast light on the significance of early infant attachment.

When children have a healthy, well-connected start to life, they have the best chance to develop and blossom. Adoptee voices are more important than ever in this era of assisted reproductive technology and surrogacy, where vulnerable and voiceless babies are being treated as consumer commodities.

For all these reasons, I have written *Light on Adoption*.

Introduction

'Every mythic hero was abandoned, and at some point they embark on a search … often it is for treasure … the treasure is the self.'

—BJ Lifton

Mythologist Joseph Campbell studied the ancient and modern-day myths of different cultures around the world, and wrote about the basic pattern evident throughout all of them. At the centre of most myths is the hero/warrior, whose journey involves three essential stages: separation, initiation and return. First the hero is taken out of their familiar environment through some problem or challenge. They are called to embark on a journey, which they may try to resist out of fear. If or when the hero answers the call to step into the unknown, they are faced with setbacks and trials during their odyssey. As they face their fears and overcome the challenges, they are transformed and rewarded. They return home with the knowledge, or treasure, that they find at the successful completion of their journey.

The popular archetypal myth of the helpless abandoned baby who succeeds in finding a path of survival is found in many folk and fairy tales; a lonely misfit faced with, and overcoming, many hardships and battles ultimately becoming victorious and finding their place within their community. How many adoptees share this classic story and are at different points on their hero's journey?

Light on Adoption includes these three stages of my life. The first stage encompasses my birth and early childhood, when I was lost in the 'fog'. The term 'fog' is commonly used these days in adoption circles, and my understanding of the 'fog' is this: it is a lack of clarity, a state of disconnection from self, confusion, and isolation. The fog is a forged and fraught place to dwell. When I was in the fog, I was hyper-vigilant, anxious, lonely and unhappy, operating out of a coping/protective trauma-based personality rather than a confident and relaxed sense of self.

From the fog I would cry out for help, but nobody heard or responded. I couldn't audibly articulate my needs—I was a grey ghost, not fully embodied. I was a lost soul. Using alcohol and drugs was a way of numbing the pain of feeling insubstantial, of not knowing who I was. I had lost myself in the fog. The fog is what I call PATSD—post adoption traumatic stress disorder.

The second stage of my life begins with my determination to find my way out of the fog.

I was in my late teens when the journey began, and it was the start of many trials and tests, encounters with allies and enemies, and a lot of learning and growth as I gradually made progress along my path.

In accordance with the mythic structure of Joseph Campbell's *The Hero's Journey*, along the way a mentor would show up for me at just the right time and place, or I would see signs and synchronicities when I needed guidance or encouragement. Every challenge, betrayal and adversary that I overcame built my strength and confidence.

With hindsight, I see my life as a search for truth, which turned out to be the truth of who I am. I had no idea when I first started on my treasure hunt that *I* was going to be the prize. The path I took weaves its way through my research, references and adoptee voices. I share some of my stories and revelations, and what has helped me over approximately thirty-five years of steadily making my way through the murk and mire of PATSD.

The third stage relates my return to 'self' and my subsequent transformation. In these last chapters of the book, I detail the lessons I learned in light of the new dawn of my awakened life, elucidating a way forward based on compassion, social justice and love.

1

Mamatoto

'In Africa we carry our children so they feel loved.'

—Irene Wambui

Mamatoto is Swahili for motherbaby, acknowledging and reflecting the concept that mother and baby are one unit rather than two separate individuals.

This primal motherbaby bond begins before birth. In the womb, baby knows mother through all its senses. Baby knows the sound of mother's voice, and can smell their mother's body. Motherbaby are emotionally attuned, and their heartbeats are in harmony. The safety and security of the womb and the baby's growing attachment to mother underpin the healthy development of the infant. In a usual post-natal progression, a newborn will have skin-to-skin contact with mother, and the baby will find its way to the breast and attach and suckle. This gentle natural continuum forms the basis for healthy attachment, which will affect all future relationships. Life outside the womb is an easy adjustment when baby is held, fed and rocked within the warm embrace and familiar smells and sounds of mother. Loving parents welcome their precious child to the world.

It is well researched and acknowledged that inadequate mother-infant relationships result in long-term adverse consequences for the child, affecting the child's cognitive and socio-emotional development, physical health, and personal relationships. The authors of *A General Theory of Love* write: 'The lack of an attuned mother is a non-event for a reptile and a shattering injury to the complex and fragile limbic brain of a mammal.'

There is no stronger bond than that of motherbaby. Nothing can substitute for this natural primal relationship. Motherbaby are joined to one another in the most intimate connection a human being can experience. Separating motherbaby is akin to a physical amputation.

There is much more to bonding than we realise. Based on electrocardiogram measurements of the energy field generated by the heart, science has discovered that heart fields interact and affect each other up to and even beyond a metre from the body.

A mother and infant's heart fields overlap in a coherent harmonic resonance of one heart to another, which begins in utero. When the baby is removed from the mother's heart field, the baby's and mother's hearts become incoherent, and coherency is only restored when the infant is brought back into an immediate adjacent relationship with the mother's heart. Once the mother's heart has lifted the baby's heart from an incoherent mode back into concord, both hearts then move into entrainment, meaning that both the mother's and baby's heart-frequency wave forms match and are in harmony. Their brain waves then also go into a coherent state and there is a perfect balance.

There is a direct dialogue between the heart and the brain. Particularly in the first nine months, the mother's realm of influence (the state of her heart) determines pre-frontal brain development.

Bonding is coherent heart-brain field entrainment between mother and infant. (It's interesting to note that for much of my life I felt that I had a broken heart; my chest area actually felt hollow.) Severing a newborn from their mother 'tears' the heart, which can feel like a hole in the soul. When motherbaby are disconnected, each feels that a piece of themselves is missing.

The sacred bond of *mamatoto* provides a firm foundation for a wholesome human life.

In the beginning …

I was in my mid-twenties when re-birthing, also known as conscious connected breathing, was in its heyday, and it was considered a direct and powerful method for healing childhood wounding, in particular trauma associated with the birth process. It was a profound period of discovery for me, as well as recovery from some of the psychological and physical effects of my birth trauma. Connected breathing had the life-changing effect of relaxing my diaphragm, allowing me to breathe fully and deeply for the first time. I also accessed feelings and somatic memories that had been hidden in my unconscious/implicit memory. In the same way that hypnosis can uncover early memories and critical experiences, re-birthing can exhume memories and feelings as far back as birth.

Here is a summary of my experience, which I wrote at the time.

'I'm floating in a feeling of warmth and oneness, cocooned by a flesh and blood, breathing body that is my capsule carrying me to earth. This living, beating entity is my vehicle and I am a part of it. I feel safe and at peace. I'm in transition, incubating and acclimatising in my fluid realm, growing and preparing inside my mothership for entry to the world outside.

'Suddenly a shockwave penetrates my languid space, and through the darkness of my cocoon comes a knowing; I know that my mother is not going to be there on my arrival.

'My whole being contracts in dread. I don't want to leave my safe and connected comfort zone, so I resist the force that's pushing me. I'm trying to hang on, but the squeezing is getting tighter and faster. I'm being pushed to my death. And then I'm engulfed by terror and rage. I know that the bond is about to break.'

My next sense is of bursting through the birth canal with rocket-fuel rage, which translated to an attitude that I would carry for much of my life, and which can be summed up in the statement: *Fuck you. I don't need anybody.* A rebel was born.

I didn't trust anyone. I was suspicious and always foretelling betrayal and rejection. I came into this world utterly alone and unconnected to anyone. Separation from my mother at birth undermined my potential to build a healthy, happy life. Like trying to build a house on sand, my development was a frail scaffold erected on shifting ground, highly susceptible to collapse.

'Calling Occupants of Interplanetary Craft'

I used to love this song by the Carpenters (and I still do). I identified with the lyrics because when I was a child, I believed that I was a lost alien observer from another planet living amongst humans. (Coincidentally, I have seen many UFOs during my life, and have had a couple of very close encounters. Maybe there's some truth to my story!).

As a child, I didn't know where I'd come from, but I knew I wasn't human. I was an outsider. I was from another place, another planet, and I had to learn to adapt to the world on Earth.

When I closed my eyes, I could see what had happened to me. I was floating in space, weightless, in my white spacesuit and helmet, securely fastened to my mothership, when suddenly the tether snapped. I saw myself tumbling, hurtling into dark, black empty space, lost, alone and terrified.

This is the shocking thing that happened to me.

I fell to Earth. I didn't know where I'd landed, or anything about the humans around me. Everything was strange. These people weren't my people. I knew nothing about them or their ways, and I had to try to blend in so they didn't realise I wasn't one of them. I had to observe and learn all about being human. It was very hard, and I was scared they would find out that I wasn't real.

There were times when I had to use my special power of invisibility because I felt safe when the humans couldn't see me. I walked around in front of them, and they couldn't tell that I was there. When I became sad and was sent to my room, or my adoptive parents were angry because I didn't get things right, I concentrated with all of my mind to call a spaceship to come and pick me up and take me back home. But they didn't come, and I had to try even harder to fit in.

The family who had taken me in were clearly struggling to make me one of their own. I knew this because I was often reminded that I wasn't good enough. My adoptive father said that he would rather have adopted chipmunks. My adoptive mother said that she wondered what her own daughter would have been like. Different from alien me, evidently. This made my terror even worse—that I would be found out as a flawed substitute human child. I had terrifying dreams where I saw my adoptive parents' three 'real' children making their way up the driveway to the front door of the house, and I had to quickly find somewhere to hide before I was exposed as an imposter.

I had to be on high alert all the time, scanning my environment and the people in it to understand what they expected of me, and how they reacted to things. It was very difficult and scary. I felt so alone, and I wished that my people would come and get me. I felt abandoned.

Not fitting in, feeling different, and a sense of not belonging are all common themes discussed in the adoptee support groups I've attended and facilitated. Some adoptees carry deep within a sense of being *like* human without actually *being* human.

Robert, aged forty-nine, said: 'I always felt very different, I felt like I was from another planet. Bonding didn't happen in my family.'

David, aged thirty-six, was told when he was ten that he was adopted, yet he said he 'always knew; I always carried the feeling of being different and not belonging'.

During my social-ecology studies, a male respondent to a survey for adoptees said: 'I might feel more real, more valid, if my origins were confirmed for me. This may sound crazy, but how can I know that I exist if I don't know how I came into existence or whence, where and when?'

And this from a woman who was also adopted: 'People said that my daughter resembled my husband more than me. This made me feel very isolated, as though I wasn't even human.'

In one support group meeting, Fiona recounted her story about not feeling fully human. Some years earlier a friend had told her about a science-fiction story she was reading. In the story there were 'real' people and 'filler' people. Fiona couldn't remember if she had spoken out loud, or had simply had the thought, but she believed she would be one of the filler people.

The immediate identification with the filler people had remained a significant memory for Fiona. When we talked more about the meaning of the memory, she said that the filler people reflected a lack of soul, and this matched her feeling of being hollow. It also spoke to her of a sense of being less important than others. Like the filler characters, she could relate to being a pawn in people's lives, the real people being the ones who made the decisions.

In *Journey of the Adopted Self*, adoptee and author BJ Lifton writes that the secrecy and suppression of genuine feelings within her adopted family caused her to feel as though she was 'someone unreal pretending to be real'. I can relate when she says that she copied the things that her friends did, and that although she looked real in photographs, she didn't feel real.

This is one of the psychological complexities of adoption that can only be understood by people who have experienced it. I felt a great sense of relief and validation when I shared this eerie sense of unreal-ness with other adoptees.

In *Blackbird*, Jennifer Lauck writes: 'It's a terrible thing to be alone when you are with other people, and especially when those other people are supposed to be your family even when they aren't, not really. That kind of being alone makes you feel wrong inside your own body, like your bones don't fit under your skin, like something inside your stomach wants to get out and fly away.'

2

Building a House on Sand

'Like the tree that puts roots deep into the clay, each of us needs the anchor of belonging in order to bend with the storms and continue toward the light.'

—John O'Donohue

Unlike the tree, I wasn't rooted to place, or the human race.

'Building a house on sand' is a metaphor for endeavouring to build a life without the solid and secure underpinning of connection and belonging. The foundations for a child's development are laid down very early in their life. A safe, protected and consistently supportive childhood forms building blocks of trust, self-value and confidence. A building is only as strong as its foundation. It is a primal imperative for a child to bond with and be nurtured by their mother and to know their biological origins and ancestry. This is the basis for the formation of the child's sense of identity and place in the world.

Over the years, people have told me directly, or inferred, that I was lucky because they didn't like their own family and used to wish that they were adopted. They felt unloved, or their father was an alcoholic, or they mention various other valid reasons for feeling unhappy in their childhood. It can feel like I'm being lectured to, that I'm being told once again that I should be grateful that I'm adopted. It always surprises me that most non-adopted people assume that I, and other adoptees, went to a better situation. They don't realise that many adoptees were raised in dysfunctional families just like those of non-adopted people.

As well as the trauma of separation at birth, there is another fundamental difference that people who weren't adopted can't understand and that's the basic lack of belonging to your clan. As dysfunctional as that clan may be, they look like each other, they know who their mother is, and they know who their father is. Biologically related people have knowledge of their family history. They have a sense of place. They have clarity about their connection to their family. They have roots. People who belong take it for granted, and understandably so, because connection to your kin and your position within a family constellation is every human being's birthright.

It's interesting to see how many people become defensive or fog over when I mention that mine wasn't a happy-ever-after story of adoption. I have seen people cross their arms when I talk about adoption. It's as though I'm talking taboo. Adoption propaganda has been so successfully implanted in people's minds that they automatically react defensively to a contradictory narrative.

Another very common response is to ask me *when* I found out that I was adopted, as if that's a crucial element in determining whether mine was a 'good' adoption or not. At this point I usually inform the enquirer that despite the age I was when I was told about being adopted, I already knew (in my somatic memory). After all, I was there when I was taken from my mother.

Growing up, I looked like a well-adjusted adoptee, meaning that ostensibly I had adapted suitably to my new conditions. I was intelligent, did well at school, and was independent, capable and composed. This concealment carried through into adulthood, where I could blend and impress in social settings, and be articulate and well presented.

Although I could keep it together in all kinds of complicated situations and hold myself with poise, underneath I lacked self-esteem, and was anxious and hyper-vigilant. I could be in emotional chaos and no one could detect it. Like many adoptees, living under the edict that I was lucky and should be grateful meant years of covering up my pain, suppressing my feelings, and portraying what was expected of me.

I had to lie in order to cooperate with the picture-perfect image of a happy adoptive family that was no different from a biologically connected one. As a master of disguise, I had no anchoring in a sense of self and place; instead, I was a counterfeit extension to a family that I felt no connection to.

A male adoptee, in his mid-fifties, told me that he has fallen and recovered countless times throughout his life. When I asked him to tell me something about his life as an adoptee, he said, 'I have been down and out, on the streets, with no money and no home, but I've always managed to climb back up and rebuild. I seem to have great resilience; friends have remarked on this. Everything is dependent on the foundation. If the foundation is weak, the building will fall down. This is a good metaphor for my life so far.'

An adoptee friend of mine spoke of his recurrent feeling that his foundations were crumbling, that he was falling into a sense of numbness, of having no substance, and worthlessness. This fall into an emotional abyss would occur within the context of a significant relationship, when he would lose his sense of connection to that person, and himself, in a critical moment where he felt there 'wasn't enough me' to sustain the relationship.

In their book, *The Psychology of Adoption*, authors David Brodinsky and Marshall Schecter write that 'connectedness to an adopted person is like water to a person in the desert'. When I look back at my own childhood, my main memory is of the pervading anguish of not belonging, and of feeling disconnected and dispirited. These feelings were compounded by the isolation of not being able to express my anxiety to anyone. It didn't matter how much material support was bestowed on me; the absence of emotional support undermined my potential for a happy childhood. Beneath the facade of the well-adjusted, acquiescent adoptee was an unhappy withdrawn child, living with a constant sense of being a flawed substitute for my adoptive mother's 'own' daughter.

When I was a child, I would stand in front of my big dressing-table mirror and stare at my reflection. I was searching for something, for some sense of connection to myself. Who was the person in the mirror? I felt no relationship to her. It was a strange and creepy feeling. I would turn my back on the mirror and then quickly turn around again to see if I could trick the reflection and catch it unawares. The image in the mirror seemed to take on a life of its own and I would run out of my room in fright.

A sense of connection (to yourself) and belonging to your clan forms the basis of a solid sense of identity. Our origins and identities are sacrosanct and enshrined in the UN convention on the rights of children: article 8 states that every child has the right to their identity, including their nationality, name and family relationships. Clearly the way adoptees have been treated violates our basic human rights.

The happy-ever-after myth of an adopted, anonymous-donor-conceived or surrogate-gestated child thriving on the abundance of love and security provided by their parents dismisses the essential elements of bonding and belonging in a human life. Disguised by a child's ability to adapt, and the development of a coping personality, the silent pain of separation trauma, loss and grief can hauntingly undermine a person's potential for intimacy and happiness into adulthood.

Belonging. Perhaps nothing in life matters more. My need to find a sense of belonging was a call to action that took me on a world trek. Enchanted Ireland and hauntingly beautiful Kenya were highlights.

3

Odyssey

'Your feet will bring you to where your heart is.'

—IRISH PROVERB

It was 1979, and I was chafing at the bit to leave home and the restrictions of my controlling adoptive parents, so when I finished high school I worked and saved solidly for about eighteen months, then bought a one-way ticket from Adelaide to London. I was eighteen. I announced my plan to my parents only a couple of weeks before my flight, and they were not impressed.

London was electric, and eclectic, a fantastic feast for my senses. The bustling streets were crowded with colourful Mohican punks wearing bullet belts, chunky buckled boots, and dripping with safety pins, metal spikes and chains. To an Adelaide girl, it was like landing on a strange planet in the centre of the universe. The place was alive, and I loved it.

I met two other Australian girls who had won a trip for two to London and they invited me to stay at their plush hotel near Hyde

Park. I then travelled around England and worked in Cornwall before taking the ferry from Holyhead to Dublin.

Landing in Ireland was like coming home. Most people had a classic Celtic complexion like me, and they had an infectious zest for life. I felt as though I'd found my tribe. I fell in love with Ireland. I was immediately enchanted by its magic, the iridescent green countryside and the music, which was an integral part of everyday life there; on the train from Dublin to Killarney I sat across from a young woman who sang out loud with the voice of an angel.

Back then, forty years ago, I was still very much in the fog: the fuzzy hazy world of post adoption traumatic stress disorder. I really was a lost soul, looking for my place in the world. More significantly, I was searching for myself. As with Joseph Campbell's *Hero's Journey*, I had left my comfort zone on a call to adventure, and Ireland was the start of my long odyssey.

Africa

One of my favourite movies is *Born Free*, the story of Joy and George Adamson, played by Virginia McKenna and Bill Travers. The lyrics of the iconic song still resonate: 'Born free, as free as the wind blows, as free as the grass grows, born free, to follow your heart.' When I was in my teens, I used to fantasise about living with the Adamsons and their pride of lions at their camp in Kora National Park. It's an interesting coincidence that I now have a friend who played an acting role in the movie of George Adamson's life in Kenya, *To Walk with Lions*.

My time in Africa was one of the radically life-changing chapters of my life. After leaving England and Ireland, I worked in Munich and saved enough to buy a one-way ticket to Nairobi, Kenya (remember the days of one-way tickets and no particular plans?). I had dreamed of going to Kenya since I was young, as an avid fan of the TV shows, *Kimba the White Lion* and *Daktari*.

I took off on a wing and a prayer, with no itinerary, no bookings, just a brimming excitement to be in the exotic land of my dreams, Africa. I was on the adventure of my life. I left freezing minus-fifteen-degree Munich and arrived in thirty-degree heat in Nairobi. I landed in the chaotic Nairobi terminal, fending off men who wanted money from me, and thinking on my feet about what to do next.

I got in a taxi and asked the driver to take me to the cheapest accommodation he knew of. He drove to the outskirts of the city and down a dirt road past ramshackle shops, open-air butchers with slabs of meat and offal on wooden trestle tables, and small tin cafes selling *mandazi*s (delicious African doughnuts).

He stopped at an old masonry building, a women's hostel, and I was met by a beautiful, buxom, affable woman. While I talked to her about accommodation, bubbling young women ogled me from a distance. They told me later that they didn't understand why I, a *mzungu* (white woman), would want to stay there. What was a *mzungu* like me doing in a place like this? Price was the main reason. It cost me the equivalent of twenty-five dollars a month for a bunk bed and two meals a day. Perfect.

It turned out to be one of the most wonderful and amazing experiences of my life.

All eyes were on me as I was shown to the large dorm, where I chose a top bunk bed and began unpacking my things. A giggling, non-verbal Ugandan girl came over and started rummaging through my stuff, which I had laid out on the bed. She found my sunglasses and put them on, beaming with delight when I said she could have them. She hardly took them off the whole time I was there, wearing them to breakfast, lunch and dinner. The other girls later told me her tragic story: her parents had been murdered in front of her and she'd never recovered from the trauma. Everyone at the hostel embraced her and made sure she was cared for.

Most of the girls staying there were attending secretarial school or doing some other type of study, and many were being supported by their sugar daddies. It was a common custom for girls to find a rich man to support their education and provide them with an allowance in exchange for companionship, dating, and perhaps a view to marriage.

My beautiful Ugandan friend, Peace, and her best friend, Sarah from Tanzania, took me under their wings. Sarah was intended to become second wife to her sugar daddy, who was a vet. One night Sarah and her man took Peace and me out to dinner. I remember my revulsion when a large platter of offal was placed on our table, to be shared. I politely nibbled on chewy, rubbery bits of whatever and tried hard to keep it down. After dinner we had a great time dancing under the stars and palm trees at the Small World nightclub.

I loved the Kenyan rhythms, and I especially loved the nights at the hostel when the girls gathered in the dining room and bashed out beats with their hands on the tables and sang their traditional songs in hypnotic harmony. Their bodies moved to the sounds so naturally, and I was amazed by the joy they felt and expressed through their music. They would fall about laughing at my attempts to move like they did!

Whenever I walked outside the hostel to get the usual *mandazi* and bottle of Fanta, I would be surrounded by children shyly pointing and calling, *'Mzungu! Mzungu!'* People would stop in their tracks and stare at me. Shades of the ugly duckling awkwardly standing out among the crowd.

One day as I walked along the dirt track toward the local market, I came across the body of a man lying in the grass beside the path. It looked like he'd been beaten to death. People were just walking by him, not stopping. The girls told me later that no one wanted to go to the police station (which was at the end of our road) in case they were interrogated or accused of the crime. I didn't understand then and still don't. Later that day I saw a woman crying next to the body.

Life seemed cheap, yet the people I met were so alive, with their colourful dress, relaxed ease and vibrant smiles. It was a complete contrast to my life at home.

One day I met a young couple at the Thornbush Cafe, who invited me to stay with them for a few days at their home on a tea plantation in Tigoni, about an hour from the city. We were on a day trip to Lake Naivasha and were driving along a narrow bitumen road through spreading acacia trees when I caught sight of a giraffe.

In my excitement I called out 'Stop!' from the back seat.

We pulled over and I leapt out of the car. Right there, only a few metres away, was a towering family of orange-and-tan giants: Mum, Dad and baby. And they didn't seem to mind me quietly standing there. I was gobsmacked by their size. It was surreal. This was wild Africa, and I was living the dream.

My new friends took me to Limuru market, a kaleidoscopic feast for the senses. I saw stunningly beautiful Masai and Kikuyu people, who looked like gods to me, so tall and statuesque, wearing brightly coloured cloths and fabulous beaded jewellery set against their flawless ebony skin. I was mesmerised.

In ignorance, I held up my little camera to capture the scene. A young Masai man confronted me, saying something in his language that was clearly, 'Put that camera *down*.' I didn't know then that some cultures believed photographs could steal your soul.

I was grateful for the generous hospitality of those lovely people who had showed me some of the natural beauty of authentic Africa, but I was happy to return 'home' to the hostel, to my warm and welcoming women; to be in their midst nourished my feminine soul.

In the evenings, I loved watching the girls braid each other's hair, twirling it into wonderful intricate patterns and bobbles that somehow just stayed in place without the need for clips or ties. One night, Peace and Sarah and a few other girls took me out to a night market and surprised me when we got there by telling me to pick out a *kanga* (a wrap-around cloth). Even though they had little money, they had done a whip-around to buy me a parting gift.

Those gorgeous girls had so little materially, but they radiated with a lightness and joy that I had never before experienced or witnessed. I was in awe of their little community, how they laughed, sang, and danced together, and looked out for each other, and above all, I was fascinated by their fellowship.

I felt so content and connected in that circle of women, even though I stood out like a white blot on a dark landscape. Life seemed so much simpler there. The month I spent with them changed me. All that I value now was first revealed to me in Africa: connection, community, authenticity, humour, fun, music, nature, acceptance and love—everything that matters. Haleluya.

4

Ireland

'When we heal ourselves, we heal the next generation that follows. Pain is passed through the family line until someone is ready to feel it, heal it and let it go'.

—S Wagner

After roaming around Europe and Kenya, I returned to Ireland. It was 1982 when my first son was born in County Tralee, when I was a naïve girl of twenty-one. I hadn't planned to get pregnant, but I accepted maternity wholeheartedly. I had never held a baby, and nor had I ever heard any pregnancy or birth stories, so I had to navigate my way through my pregnancy as best I could without any ready information to draw upon, and with scant support.

My partner and I were living in a lovely historic two-storey cottage in the countryside about ten kilometres outside Killarney, County Kerry. It was beautiful there. I remember my washing line was in a paddock, occupied by a cranky horse that liked to nip me when I wasn't looking, and the thick hedgerows were full of big juicy blackberries that I baked into sticky purple pies.

I have fond memories of scouring the nearby spinney for wood and dragging branches home to chop for the fire, and making nettle and elderberry wine and seeing the brown bottles slowly bubbling on the sunny windowsills. There were also warm pub nights listening to traditional musicians jamming by a roaring open fire, wild nights dancing on tables (before I was pregnant), and picnics in bluebell glades by the lake. But probably my best memory was of a *ceili* we had one night at our cottage with a local fiddle player, bodhran and whistle. We set danced in our little lounge room on bouncing floorboards until seven in the morning. It was the best *craic*!

But I was also isolated, being pregnant and living in the countryside with no car, and spending a lot of time alone when my partner was at work. Living with an abusive narcissist made me feel even more alone and unhappy. Although back then I didn't know that I was with a malignant narcissist because I had never known a man who wasn't. My partner and my adoptive father were of the same ilk. And you don't know what you don't know.

Eire, forty years ago, was staunchly Catholic. I had never been immersed in such a religious culture before, so it came as a shock when people in the village, who had previously been friendly to me, cut me off cold when it became known that I was pregnant and unmarried. I felt hurt when people I would have said hi to in the street put their heads down and walked on. Much like the forced-adoption years in Australia, young single mothers were cruelly stigmatised and ostracised in conventional Catholic rural Ireland at that time.

Little did I know that worse was yet to come. What I now know, with hindsight, is that an uncannily similar scenario to my birth mother's and my own birth story was gradually unfolding.

I had wanted a home birth, but it was proving very difficult to find a doctor who would support me. I was very much on my own in my pregnancy and planning. One day I hitchhiked to neighbouring County Tralee to see yet another doctor to try to get him on board. Running to catch up to a car that had stopped to give me a lift may have triggered the start of my labour that night.

Next day I was at home alone as usual and my discomfort continued. I didn't know I was in labour. My due date was still some weeks away. I called the doctor, who came over, and after I described my contractions, he said I probably had a urinary tract infection and gave me some antibiotics. What a quack. After he'd gone, I lay in bed all day with increasingly painful contractions. I look back at that time with sadness and compassion for the vulnerable naïve young woman I was, dealing with so much with little practical support and zero emotional support.

That evening I was taken to hospital in an ambulance. It was all so unnecessarily dramatic. I was taken not to the hospital I preferred, but to the closer, notorious hospital I had wanted to avoid. The nurse in the ambulance assured me that my partner would be allowed to stay with me throughout the birth. This was not a given back in those days in Ireland, and it was something that was very important to me. However, not only was my partner banned from the labour ward, but I was also treated with utter disdain, threatened with sedation if I didn't 'shut up' and stop resisting. I was dragged across the floor into the labour ward by two hefty nurses as I screamed that I had been lied to and wanted my partner present. I was humiliated, laughed at, and told to 'get on with it'. It was a nightmare.

My son was taken from me straight after his birth and put into an incubator. This was senseless, because he was a healthy seven pounds and babies need to be with their mothers, not separated and alone. As I lay in the ward bed, unaided and sobbing my heart out, a kind woman came over and asked me what the matter was. Immediately one of the bullies from the labour ward approached and, in her strong Kerry accent, said, 'Leave her alone, she's a naughty little girl.'

The next month was agonising beyond description. I was being punished, just as my birth mother would have been punished for having a baby out of wedlock. I wasn't allowed into the nursery to see and touch my baby; all I could do was to watch him from the doorway. I was heartbroken without my baby; all I wanted was to hold him.

It's painful remembering this time. I was young, vulnerable and out of my depth. I was treated like trash. I had no support. It's hard for people who know me today to believe that I didn't stand up and fight, or just take my baby out of there. Of course I would do that now, but what many people don't realise is how far I've come from being a troubled and disempowered young person to being the kick-ass warrior woman I am today! I've had to build my strength over time, brick by brick.

I endured a month of torturous separation from my baby. He had become sick, which was the hospital's reason for keeping him there.

He wouldn't have become ill if he had been where he belonged. I wept every day until I brought him home. When he finally did come back to me, the little guy was drowsy and colicky. I was a new mum with no one at my back, trying to cope with a crying baby at home alone.

My son has had many corresponding issues with adoptees, including anxiety, depression, attachment and emotional-regulation problems. This is a clear case of multi-generational trauma, stemming from my birth mother, and perhaps even further back, including his separation from me, and his separation from his own son.

My lived experience has taught me how critically important it is to honour and support the natural birth and post-natal continuum. Whether it's surrogacy, adoption or any form of baby selling, separating babies at birth is inhuman and immoral. The baby suffers and is radically fractured, which has life-long consequences. When will we stop wilfully inflicting such horrendous heartbreak upon vulnerable newborns?

5

Mental Health

'The strongest people are not those who show strength in front of the world but those who fight and win battles that others do not know anything about.'

—Jonathan Harnisch

How many adoptees have undiagnosed mental ill health? In a 2014 study published in *Comprehensive Psychiatry*, the National Epidemiologic Survey on Alcohol and Related Conditions (NESARC) conducted a study that compared lifetime prevalence rates and odds ratios of anxiety, mood, and psychotic disorders in adopted-versus-non-adopted people in a nationally representative sample. It was concluded that adoptees in a large sample from the general population had a higher prevalence of several lifetime mood and anxiety disorders compared with non-adoptees.

Physician and author Gabor Maté describes mental illness as normal responses to abnormal circumstances. A lot of attention is paid to mental health these days; it has become mainstream. But in the sixties and seventies when I was growing up, mental health was rarely mentioned. If you walked and talked and looked normal, you were fine. People were told to 'get on with it', 'put on a brave face', or, my favourite, 'eat a spoonful of cement and toughen up'. Now, of course, we're all versed in the importance of asking, 'Are you okay?'

When I was a child, anxiety and depression weren't words used in everyday vernacular, unlike today, but my adoptive family was a breeding ground (pardon the unintended pun) for mental ill health. It's ironic that mental health was never mentioned in my house, because I was growing up in a severely mentally unhealthy family. No one in my family ever asked anyone else if they were okay, but every member of my adoptive family had mental-health issues. Anxiety, depression, narcissism and aggression—we were all struggling. 'Tortured' is an appropriate word to sum up my mental health as a child. It's no exaggeration to say that I was in discomfort daily. I was frightened, sad and confused.

Growing up in a dysfunctional adoptive family is difficult to describe, but I'll try. We were five unrelated, unbonded, very different individuals, in looks and character. We bore no resemblance to one another. We had no common relatives, no genetic mirroring, and no birth stories. Saddest of all, there was very little loving compassion in our house.

Rather, we were actors in a play, suppressing our true feelings and pretending that we were a related family. We were like cardboard cutouts of the real thing. Add to this flawed script a sadistic, controlling adoptive father; a violent acting-out adoptive brother; and an oppressed, depressed adoptive mum. We were a household of hurt people who, inadvertently or not, hurt each other.

I recall my parents' friends, who had also emigrated from England and lived in the neighbouring suburb. Like us, they were a family of five, two boys and a girl, but unlike us they all looked like each other. They were tubby, round-faced and rosy-cheeked people, with similar noses. They reminded me of the TV show, *The Darling Buds of May*, where the mother is ensconced in the kitchen making and baking comfort food in grand quantities. There were regular knees-up parties where no one was allowed to stay seated when the Mexican hat dance or 'Zorba the Greek' was played. 'Uncle' Ernie used to play the spoons, and sozzled adults swung each other around the lounge room with gay abandon. Their family recipe had the magic ingredients of connectedness, love and fun. There was joy at their house.

In stark contrast, my family was seething with tension and trepidation, rigid rules and Victorian values. Authenticity was not part of our family vocabulary, and joy was an unknown verve. My experience of growing up in an adopted family was a sad study in sadism and suppression.

I had no idea how dysfunctional my adoptive family was until I was well into my forties, when I was sharing some of the lowlights of my childhood with a friend who is a mental-health nurse. She was aghast. She told me that nowadays my brothers and I would have been removed by child-protection services.

Adoptees who have had lifetime troubles with mental health must be one of the most unseen, unheard and overlooked sectors of society.

Dysthymia

Dysthymia is a term for chronic low-grade depression, and the disorder has become so much a part of people that they believe that is simply how life is. I've heard many adoptees over the years speak of an underlying melancholy. Like many of us, my upbeat personality belied my persistent sense of unhappiness, a deep dark underground stream of sorrow. I didn't know that this had a name: dysthymia.

It used to be hard work putting on a brave face and a bright side. I was the funny kid in primary school, with a little entourage following me around the playground laughing at my jokes. But it always felt like an effort, like I was faking it. No one knew the truth, that inside I felt out of sorts and anxious, and desperately wanted to be accepted.

Years ago, in the small town where I used to live, I met a Jewish woman who was vivacious, warm and generous. She was very encouraging when I told her about writing this book and offered to help me in any way she could. She was a powerhouse of positivity, who conceived of and co-created a wonderful festival that showcased different religions, spiritual faiths and rituals. I don't think it had ever been done before and it was a great success. I loved it, and everyone else seemed to love it as well. A short time later, this beautiful woman killed herself.

I couldn't reconcile her suicide with her effervescent personality, and her outstanding achievement with the award-winning inaugural interfaith festival. To this day, I wonder what was going on behind the scenes in her heart and mind. Did she suffer from dysthymia?

Why did she take the drastic step of taking her life? Who would have known that this bright creative woman was struggling mentally?

Humans can become so adept at covering pain and presenting a strong front, and I think adoptees in particular are masters at this. Adoptees are so good at adaptation that we are often called chameleons. Like chameleons, we are skilled at adjusting our behaviour to please, to present what is expected and accepted, and to blend in. I've had a lot of practice at blending in and wearing a false mask, beginning with the charade of my 'model' adoptive family.

Unsettled

Feeling unsettled was a bane in my life; moving house, getting up out of my chair for yet another cup of tea, juggling a head full of swirling thoughts like balls in the air, none of them landing. Living a zigzag life makes it very difficult to move forward.

Just as I hadn't known that my anxiety had a name, I didn't know that my inability to focus and stay still also had a name: attention deficit hyperactivity disorder (ADHD). In an article titled 'Uncomfortable Truths About the ADHD Nervous System', the author wrote that those with an ADHD nervous system might as well have been born on a different planet. So not only did being adopted cause me to feel like an alien, I actually had an extra-terrestrial nervous system!

According to the Centre for Disease Control, 9–11 percent of children are thought to have ADHD, but for adoptees it can be as high as 20–30 percent. Gabor Maté says that ADHD is a natural mechanism to deal with stress. If someone is unable to leave a stressful situation physically, their mind will disconnect them as protection from the impact of the stress.

When I was at school, I would stare out of the window and go on a magic-carpet daydream. It was the only way I could escape being fixed in a chair. My report cards often said that I was a dreamer. My adoptive mother regularly called me a scatterbrain. I used to tune out, a lot.

I look at old black-and-white photos of five-year-old me with glazed eyes gazing off into the distance. To this day I'm absentminded and have difficulty focusing (which is probably why it took me eighteen years to finish this book). My hypersensitivity to distraction, even the slightest noise, has made it difficult for me to complete tasks. I have lived with ADHD, but it was never diagnosed.

A hundred tangled thoughts crowding my mind, taking me in all different directions at the same time, can be very distressing and debilitating. It can either immobilise or hyper-mobilise me. I would use drugs and alcohol to calm my brain enough to be productive. Distraction and self-medication are ways to leave without going anywhere. Drinking and drug taking are an unsustainable escape.

I've regretted moving house so many times as it has always been an expensive stress and it takes so much time to resettle. I once moved three times in one year, which took me to the edge of a nervous breakdown. In one of my journal entries, I wrote these words: 'I have to force myself to be stable and build my centre/ my foundation. The roaming has to come to an end. I want the fragments of my self to stop floating in space, or being swept up in the slipstreams of other people's lives. I need to gather myself in and consolidate, anchor, strengthen, build power, become a force, instead of a will-o'-the wisp.'

Moving is a common theme in the lives of adoptees. Many adoptees become habitual movers; some will move every year for years. I have heard a common complaint that moving is extremely taxing, stressful and hated, yet it seems unavoidable.

It's as if there is a literal absence of roots to keep some of us supported and steady.

But is it any wonder, when moving has been an involuntary action since our birth?

The first experience of life for many adoptees is moving—moving from the homeland of the womb to the intermediate and clinical environment of a hospital, then perhaps to a foster home or children's home, and then another unfamiliar environment of an adoptive home. Adoptees were infant migrants, who have, in many cases, been uprooted and transplanted at least three times during the first few months of their lives.

Post-adoption traumatic stress disorder (PATSD)

You won't find this term in a diagnostic psychiatric manual, as it's one I have coined to more adequately acknowledge and describe the exceptional and catastrophic consequences of natal amputation. Living with post-adoption traumatic stress disorder (PATSD) can be a silent struggle. It has seriously impacted my own life, and countless thousands of adoptees' lives. Claiming the reality of my

PATSD, and understanding its insidious influence on my life, has been a revelation.

I have gradually become clearer about the causes and manifestations of PATSD, and the symptoms include:

- Panic attacks
- A feeling of emptiness
- Obsessive worrying
- Being easily startled
- Emotional dysregulation
- Feeling like a misfit
- Separation anxiety
- Intense anger
- Binge behaviour
- Disconnection with and disassociation from self, other people or the environment
- Mistrust in relationships
- Depression
- Low self-esteem and self-worth
- Pattern of leaving places
- Distancing/withdrawing
- Boundary issues
- Drug and alcohol addiction
- Intense grief over minor losses
- Acute rejection sensitivity
- Emotional numbness/dissociation from feeling
- Hyper-vigilance
- No internal anchor to self
- Pre-emptive (rejection) strikes

When we are triggered into an episode of PATSD, our anxiety takes us out of the present moment, and instead we re-experience a destabilising memory of helplessness, panic and loss. Anxiety is the activation of the energy experienced during the original overwhelming event. When we are threatened, our body instinctively generates a lot of energy to help us defend ourselves against the threat.

An obvious manifestation of my own PATSD is how easily I am startled. If someone suddenly appears in front of me or speaks unexpectedly from behind me, my whole body reacts in terror, and my bloodcurdling screams can cause the person to literally run for cover. Any unexpected movement, noise or touch can trigger a hyper-reaction in me. This is a typical example of a nervous system on high alert.

The process of taking a baby at birth and holding them in limbo—in my case, for six weeks—before giving them to complete strangers creates a set of compounding stresses that will have a lifelong effect on the infant's development, and physical and mental health. High levels of the stress hormone cortisol in response to birth trauma are compounded by the absence of the child's mother, and the lack of soothing of the newborn's distress. Elevated cortisol levels cannot be lowered without adequate soothing.

Jack Shonkoff, paediatrician and professor of child health and development at Harvard University, explains that 'extreme, long-lasting stress in the absence of support to buffer the effects of a heightened stress response can produce damage and weakening of bodily and brain systems. This can lead to diminished physical and mental health throughout a person's lifetime'.

The prolonged anguish of adoptees who live with PATSD is inestimable and untold. Many will simply be unaware that pervasive problems in their lives and relationships are a consequence of separation trauma.

In the mid-eighties, I knew there was something seriously wrong with me when depression and anxiety became a continuous undercurrent that permeated my daily life. I still remember the moment I made the decision to search for the cause of my problems.

I was parenting my two very young children under the tyranny of a narcissistic partner. I was depressed for days at a time, physically unwell (I had conjunctivitis for months), and chronic fatigue. I also had bouts of peripheral neuropathy, and simply functioning day to day was at times an excruciating effort.

I needed to make sense of my sickness and sorrow, and so my quest began. I started by seeking help from a psychiatrist, who was utterly useless. After that I saw a variety of clinicians and counsellors, none of whom had a clue that adoption was a core issue worth investigating. Unbelievably, they all seemed to have zero knowledge of the critical attachment violation and associated trauma that had occurred at the beginning of my life. And I certainly didn't know.

In the early 2000s I worked as a massage therapist in a rehab retreat that offered cognitive behavioural therapy, healthy food, and massage treatments to people with addiction issues and depression. During that time, I massaged people who were adoptees and who were not making progress in the program. When I talked about adoption and shared my story with them, it became obvious that the idea of adoption being a possible issue in their lives was a foreign notion to them. I knew that what they needed was a compassionate ear, someone to really listen to their experiences and validate their feelings. As a fellow adoptee and counsellor, I was able to do that, but many health professionals are completely unaware of the fundamental impact of birth trauma and adoption in adoptees' lives.

In a society where the realities of adoption are still conveniently overlooked in favour of the facile fairy tale that acquiring parents prefer to believe, PATSD brings attention to the taboo truth. Most non-adopted people can't connect trauma with adoption due to the prevailing and overriding narrative of rescue and redemption. I remember walking my dogs alongside another regular dog walker and we got talking about adoption and birth trauma. He stopped in his tracks and turned to me, and with an incredulous tone said: 'What? Do you mean that it's a trauma for the baby as well as the mother?'

The child's perspective is most often overlooked in conversations I hear in the media regarding adoption and surrogacy. The voices and desires of procuring parents are predominant and paramount. People believe that they are somehow *entitled* to acquire a child, and if that means tearing a newborn from a surrogate mother, or purchasing a baby from an online baby market, so be it. Whatever it takes.

There is no consideration given to the possibility that a baby separated at birth is a distressed baby without a secure start in life, and will most likely grow into an insecure adult who is disconnected from their authentic self. The best definition of authentic self that I've found is Dr Gabor Maté's description: 'Authenticity is knowing how you feel, being in touch with your body and expressing who you are.'

For most of my life I didn't know who I was. I had no idea. My feelings were a prohibited part of me. Having no connection to myself, led me into many unhappy, disrespectful, cruel situations and relationships. I may as well have been holding a placard that said: *I'm vulnerable. I have no boundaries. Come and get me.* When I first heard the term 'trauma-based partner picking', I immediately identified.

With the right kind of support, we can heal. Healing PATSD requires understanding, support, validation and compassion.

After years of struggling alone and searching for help, the most powerful healing resources I found have been Voice Dialogue, which I talk about later, and my relationships with people who have openly and actively listened with genuine interest. An adoption-informed therapist has been invaluable. Authors of *The Power of Showing Up,* Daniel Siegel and Tina Bryson, summarise the vital needs of a child by the four S's: the need to feel safe, soothed, seen, and secure. Many adoptees have been callously denied these important essentials when they were at their most vulnerable and formative, but it's now possible to find the right people and the right places to have these needs met. Adoptee support groups, and a therapist who was also an adoptee, moved mountains for me because I was supported to feel safe, soothed, seen and secure.

6

Rejection

'Rejection—and the fear of rejection—is the biggest impediment we face to choosing ourselves.'

—JAMES ALTUCHA

For anyone, rejection can feel like a knife in the heart. For adoptees, it's a chainsaw. Rejection, disconnection, separation = pain. Hyper-vigilance for even the slightest hint that I would be rejected or abandoned by my partner would involve high levels of anxiety. The most extreme reaction (in my late teens) to perceived abandonment by my boyfriend was to cut my wrists.

In the realm of relationships, my PATSD would unravel me regularly. Looking for evidence that I was unloved, and anticipating and re-experiencing the terror of being abruptly cut off from my love/life line (from connection to mother) activated seesawing stress levels in me that at times were extremely debilitating. I've lost days when I've been too stressed or depressed to function, over real or imagined rejection. Being pleasing and agreeable was one strategy that I would use to try and ensure that I wouldn't be abandoned.

Rejection sensitive dysphoria (RSD), which describes extreme emotional sensitivity to criticism or rejection, whether real or perceived, explains what many adoptees experience. This condition is an underlying, insidious disorder that plagues millions of adopted people who cannot achieve lasting bonded connection to an intimate partner. This is still a largely unacknowledged tragedy of birth trauma and broken attachment.

A prevalent adoptee pattern is to repeatedly re-experience rejection, sometimes unintentionally brought about by over-attaching, rejecting and testing behaviour ('Show how much you love me') or by reading too much into the words and actions of others, 'proving' to us that they don't really care.

We can suddenly sever a relationship with the cutting finality of a guillotine. Conversely, we can stay in unhealthy relationships too long, trying to make them work and unable to face loss.

There's also a classic adoptee plot twist, which involves rerunning a self-perpetuating loop where the adoptee is the rejecter in an attempt to prevent being rejected; in other words, making a pre-emptive strike. I know, it's a mind bender. But in the coping mind of the adoptee, anticipating rejection by getting in first can save us the pain of being rejected. This is a common compulsion that wreaks havoc in many adoptees' relationships. The usual outcome is to feel, once again, heartbroken, grief stricken and alone.

It's taken me a long time to learn how to manage my reactions to perceived rejection. Knowing that relinquishment/abandonment is the underlying influence helps to put reactions into perspective. Not taking things so personally and stepping back for a more objective viewpoint is important.

Another practice I've found helpful when flooded with separation anxiety is to check with my inner child and dialogue with her. Through soothing inner dialogue, my inner parent can comfort my vulnerable inner child, with calming, compassionate words of understanding. This can take a while. I may have to lie down and put my hands on my heart, belly or brow, and consciously breath deeply and slowly. Once my anxiety has dissipated I can gradually come up with a plan that will reassure my inner child that all will be okay; my inner parent lets her know that safety, care and protection are my priorities. In this way I take responsibility for looking after the part of me that was abandoned and neglected in the past.

When we become aware of a pattern of painful problematic events, we will see that they are like signposts or steppingstones that lead us back to the original event. We can ask ourselves when we last felt this way, i.e. betrayed, abandoned and rejected. By following a theme of repetitious destabilising times in our lives we can trace back to the original experience.

Separation trauma

The trauma of maternal separation at birth is difficult to trace because it happened right at the beginning of life. We have no conscious episodic memory of the event. We can't recall and verbalise what happened to us, because the memory is stored in our limbic/emotional brain. As Bessel Van Der Kolk asserts, 'The body keeps the score.'

There's an abandoned baby within every adoptee, and when something happens that reminds us of our original traumatic experience of abandonment, the embedded painful emotions are resurrected.

Another way back to a causal event is via the body. I had to work through a lot of somatic feelings and reactions to understand that patterns in my relationships stemmed from birth trauma. Rebirthing was my first unearthing of the origin of my injury.

A young man in his thirties had been a premature baby separated from his mother at birth and left alone in an incubator for several weeks. Throughout his life he had replayed a scenario where he became overly attached to his girlfriend (attachment disorder). His fear of being abandoned caused him to be controlling and jealous. He was afraid that another man would intervene and take his girlfriend from him.

This pattern initially revealed itself with his first girlfriend, when he was a young teenager. His girlfriend took off with his mate, perhaps because he had inadvertently pushed her away by his behaviour. He retreated to his bed for days, lying in his darkened bedroom medicating himself with prescription drugs. In this way he returned to a feeling of safety and comfort similar to the womb environment.

This man was caught in a perpetual loop of re-wounding situations, and no health professional had been able to help him. No one had even identified that birth trauma was a causal issue for him. Instead, he was repeatedly prescribed antidepressants and sedatives.

It's disheartening that mainstream mental-health modalities do not adequately address and help people who suffer from the aftermath of separation trauma. Birth trauma and mother loss is responsible for a multitude of mental and behavioural disorders, addictions and self-harming actions. Both adoptees and incubator babies have experienced the sudden separation from their mother. Their first relationship ended in a cold instant. This trauma serves as a blueprint for future relationships, so it's not surprising that many adult adoptee relationships end in a similar way.

Interestingly, my own love relationships have been with either physically or emotionally (or both) unavailable men. Feeling excluded and alone has been a recurrent theme throughout my past relationships.

In my opinion, relationship problems such as fear of abandonment, attachment issues, emotional dysregulation and shame are some of the most severe and hidden consequences of forced adoption. Many adoptees, and birth mothers, have opted for a life of aloneness because they have put relationships in the too-hard basket. I know of women who gave up on love and marriage and having any subsequent children after the loss of their babies to adoption. A friend, whose baby was adopted, decided there and then, as she walked away from the hospital, that she would never have another child. Unresolved feelings of grief, shame and self-blame can seriously undermine opportunities for healthy loving relationships.

The unseen wounds and scars of separation trauma are pervasive and perplexing, and need exposure to the light in order to heal.

Countless adoptees have endured a painful childhood and beyond, with no assistance. Having had an experience of living with an invisible and unattended injury, there is nothing more heart-rending to me than witnessing the complete disregard for a distressed being, human or animal, abandoned in their suffering.

Bali Star

One year my daughter and I went to Bali on holiday. Bali is an island of contrasts; of beauty and warm hospitality as well as pollution and poverty. As animal-rights activists, we were confronted by animal neglect and cruelty. We fed starving dogs and cats as we travelled, and we became involved with BAWA, the animal welfare association in Ubud, which works tirelessly to treat dogs and cats rescued from Bali streets.

One day, on a group cycling trip from Kintamani, we came across a small dog dragging her paralysed back legs along the road. My daughter and I hit the brakes and swung over to the side of the road. We were horrified. We found out later that she had been run over, and had a broken spine and displaced hips. Her limp hind legs and paws had been worn to the bone from days of scraping along the ground. Her little face was crawling with fleas, and her deformed body was terribly thin from starvation. When I approached her, she growled at me with a look of madness in her eyes.

My daughter and I noticed that we had stopped near a village *warung* (cafe), so we quickly walked over to buy some chicken and rice to feed her. She dragged herself over to us as if she knew we were going to help her. She ate voraciously, and when she'd finished we lifted her little twisted body into a cardboard box. A woman told us that she had witnessed the dog being run over by a truck several days earlier. Like many Balinese who regard dogs as unclean and unwelcome, she had observed the suffering dog with indifference.

A support vehicle was following our group of riders, and I asked the driver to help me get the dog some emergency care from BAWA in Ubud. After spending a heartbreaking few hours at the clinic while our frail little 'Bali Star' was examined, we were given the predictable prognosis that her injuries were so severe that she would need to be euthanised.

During the long hour that it took for the vet to get clearance to put her to sleep, I held her little face in my hand, watching the fleas swarming over her head and eyes as I spoke to her gently, telling her what a beautiful and brave dog she was. I was dripping sweat and tears as I focused solely on giving her as much love and support as I could in her final hour. Her trembling fear gave way to a relaxed calm, and then her face felt heavy in my hand as the lethal injection took effect.

Back in Australia, I reflected on this experience. I thought back over my life and the many times that I had encountered and rescued animals in need of help. I thought about the other bike riders in our group who had seen the distressed dog but cycled past, and I remembered the woman in our group who later hugged and thanked me for stopping to help.

I thought about my heartbreak over animal neglect and suffering, none more confronting and agonising to witness as the acute anguish of our precious Bali Star. I realised that for me the most painful part of her story was the fact that she'd been ignored for *days*. In that time no one had gone to her aid, even though she was dragging her injured body around in full view. She was amongst people yet completely alone in her pain and misery. I find this kind of neglect absolutely incomprehensible.

I thought about why I feel so deeply saddened to see people turn a blind eye to creatures in desperate need. Why had I felt compelled to stop when others saw her and rode on by? I knew it was because I could relate to the agony of being alone, unseen and unaided, of having no compassionate witness, no validation, and no loving kindness when experiencing trauma and torment. I recalled those desolate years of being among others and my pain being completely unnoticed.

Many adoptees are drawn to help and rescue those who are vulnerable and in need of an advocate. What doesn't kill you makes you kinder. The Dalai Lama said, 'My religion is very simple. My religion is kindness.' Imagine a world where kindness was everyone's religion.

7

Invisibility

> 'Your need for acceptance can make you invisible in this world. Don't let anything stand in the way of the light that shines through this form. Risk being seen in all of your glory.'
>
> —Jim Carrey

Adoptees, rather than being warmly welcomed into this world, surrounded by smiling happy people, were born into a cold sterile hospital environment in secrecy and concealment. We were a scandalous outcome of immoral conduct. Our mothers were sent away to have their babies in seclusion to avoid the shame and stigma of their sin. We were hidden right from the start.

To be spared the stigma of our shameful beginnings we were given to 'deserving and respectable' people, people who needed us in order to feel whole and happy. Our wholeness and happiness wasn't the priority. We were treated as a commodity: taken from one place, trafficked and transferred to another. Our place was with our mother. How could we possibly emerge from such an upheaval with a solid presence in our world?

For much of my life I have felt invisible. I used to feel that my presence had no impact on the people around me. I didn't think I mattered. If I was with a group of people at a dinner party, or at a friend or partner's family gathering, I would be the silent one in the background.

I felt invisible in my adoptive family—unseen and unheard. I was an extension of my adoptive parents, a clean slate on which they could superimpose their model child. I strived to be the picture-perfect presentation of the dream daughter they couldn't have.

After my adoptive mother said to me, 'I wonder what my own daughter would have been like,' I had the distinct sense that I was an inferior substitute for her ideal daughter. The dreams and expectations she had of her idealised daughter were a vague ever-presence in my childhood, and so was the ethereal sense of my birth mother, who was the proverbial invisible elephant in the room. I was acutely aware that no matter how hard I tried I would never be good enough. The real me was unseen, and therefore never fleshed out.

Combined with a complete lack of physical mirroring and genetic markers, I was utterly unconnected and alone. I felt like a hollow ghost. Nothing about my family, or even myself, felt real, solid or safe.

Recently I heard the moving and tender story of Martin Pistorious, who suffered from locked-in syndrome and wrote about his experiences in his book, *The Ghost Boy*. He became imprisoned inside his body, unable to move or communicate, but he had full awareness. He talked about the people who looked through and around him because on the surface he appeared to be in a vegetative state. He talked about his agonising helplessness, the boredom and loneliness of his isolation, and also how he was abused in his vulnerability by staff in the care home in which he lived. He wrote about the dark abyss of despair.

I felt so sad for his situation, thinking about how he suffered alone for so long, in silence and neglect, with no love and kindness offered. I reflected on Martin's unimaginable experience, and although I did not have the temerity to compare my suffering to his, I could still relate on some level. I related to his invisibility.

Throughout my childhood no one saw my internal pain, and no one validated or comforted me. I felt emotionally locked in, and, like Martin Pistorius, I too felt like a transparent spectre in a world of real people. I would regularly fall into my own dark abyss throughout my life because I couldn't express, and no one could see my torment. Later in my life, when Joe, my partner, died and I experienced the emotional and physical agony of loss, I remembered that as a child I had experienced that same pain. I had lived with an indiscernible and chronic infirmity.

An enduring memory of my invisibility comes from when I was probably five or so, when my mother and her friends were having afternoon tea in the lounge room. I remember walking around the room in front of them as they chatted, and I was convinced they couldn't see me. As I got older, I used my invisibility to my advantage. I could shrink and fade in social settings and disappear into the background familiarity, comfort and safety of not being seen.

A friend of mine once told me that she had seen me withdraw and become ghost-like when in a group situation. When I did that, I would feel myself shrink and become insignificant. If I wanted to leave a party, I would silently slip away and no one would notice, or so I thought.

My invisibility became a theme throughout my adult relationships with mainly narcissistic and/or dismissive, avoidant men who disregarded my needs and perspectives. These men were emotionally or physically unavailable, or both, and were so self-absorbed that they were incapable of reciprocal relationships.

It's no wonder that I chose men who couldn't see me or hear my point of view; after all, I had been taught, and believed deep down, that I was unimportant and unworthy. The subliminal message that I didn't matter was reinforced over and over again in my relationships. I felt repeatedly neglected, diminished and hurt. Many of my defensive and angry reactions came from my sense of (like the song) 'what about me', and were usually followed by a *'Fuck you'*.

But I always forgave my partners and stuck around in the hope that they would one day love, respect and appreciate me. However, this would never be the case until I changed my internal programming, and until I spent the time to find and flesh myself out, in the process making myself both visible and audible—*pour moi*.

Invisibility is a relational wound brought about by not being seen, listened to and responded to. Having had no one in my childhood who was attuned to me, I had to learn to attune to myself. I achieved this by asking myself how I was feeling, or what I needed in that moment, or by calming myself when I felt anxious. My therapist suggested that I imagine a scared child in front of me. What would I do? Would I hold that child and sympathise, and let her know that she was safe and protected in my arms, that everything was okay?

If we adoptees are able to relax into the safety and security of our own caring attendance, just like a loving mother or father with their child, we will develop a more solid sense of ourselves. It's our responsibility to self-soothe, to do what makes us happy, to accept or refuse what we want or don't want in our world. We need to ask ourselves what we want to do, not just today, or tomorrow, but more broadly, with our one precious life. Find a way to validate, respect and appreciate ourselves. It's up to us to give ourselves the reassurance and confidence to know that we do matter.

Sharie Stines (PsyD) says, 'How do you heal from being invisible? You have to learn how to "claim your space" here on Earth. You have to own your right to exist, to breathe, to make mistakes, to have an opinion, to want, to need, to demand.'

8

Grief

*'Our sorrows and wounds are healed only
when we touch them with compassion.'*

—BUDDHA

In the book *Birth Bond*, the authors state that loss is the fundamental ground upon which the event of adoption is built. Relinquishing mothers lost all trace of their children, along with the sanction to mourn their loss. They were expected to forget their experience of childbirth and carry on with their lives. Due to the secrecy and stigma surrounding the birth of their babies they couldn't speak about their loss and process their feelings.

Adoptees lost our mothers, our sense of safety and security, and our entire family history and original identity, yet we weren't encouraged or supported to express the grief that resulted from these profound losses.

And what about adoptive parents who adopted due to infertility? They suffered the loss of conceiving their own biological children.

Did they fully express their grief? I know that my adoptive mother didn't. She was told to just accept her lot and move on with her life.

When someone dies, there is a funeral, with cards, condolences and flowers. Sympathy and support are offered from friends and family, who acknowledge the loss and who understand there will be a period of grieving. Grieving is expected and respected. In contrast, adoption denies the immense losses suffered by all parties.

Adoptees had to silently endure our grief and make believe that all was well in our new family even if it wasn't. And to add insult to injury, we were given the message that 'it's a *good* thing your mother is not there for you, is dead to you'. Our grief was overridden with: 'You are lucky that your mother loved you so much she gave you away to a respectable loving family.' This is called gaslighting, meaning that your reality is not your reality; it's what we tell you is reality.

The insidious and pervasive burden of loss and grief in my adoptive family was invisible to the people around us and to society in general, but we all felt it. We were marinating in a morass of unexpressed grief. Adoption's cruel charade sentenced the cast of my adoptive family to decades of depression, aggression, addiction, disconnection and loneliness.

Kenneth Doka, who wrote the book *Disenfranchised Grief*, says that when loss and grief cannot be openly acknowledged, publicly mourned or socially supported, it becomes 'disenfranchised', and therefore difficult to resolve.

We cannot come to terms with our losses when we do not grieve them, and in order to fully grieve, we first need to accept the reality of those losses. We cannot grieve under a mantle of denial. We cannot love and receive love wholeheartedly when our hearts still carry grief. We need to feel the pain and express it, ideally in a safe and supportive environment. If we do not or cannot move through and beyond our grief, we will remain frozen in an incomplete stage of the grief cycle.

The grief-cycle model includes such feelings as sadness, guilt, anger, numbness and hopelessness, in varying order and intensity. When feelings are repressed, depression is likely to result. Depression is like a heavy blanket shrouding a person's grief and their potential to be happy and joyous. Unresolved grief creates a barrier to loving connection and intimacy.

A friend once framed a rhetorical question that illustrated the assumption that I think many people make. He said, 'Surely, if adoptive parents want and love their child, and provide for them, wouldn't that be enough?' I informed my friend that the reality of adoption is far more complex than the common simplistic notion of the ever-loving adoptive family.

In an interesting piece of magical thinking, many people believe that adoptive families contain even more love than biological families. This idea suggests that by waiting and anticipating for so long, adoptive parents have accumulated an abundance of love to bestow on their longed-for adopted child. This is yet another aspect of the mythical adoptive family: that their cup of love runneth over and conquers all.

Of course, the truth is that some adoptive families can be dysfunctional, just like biological families, plus the adopted baby has been through a fundamentally shattering separation trauma. My point to my friend was that the unresolved grief in my adoptive family precluded the transmission of love. No amount of 'love' bestowed on me would have penetrated my heavy heart. If I had been supported in my grieving, if I had had compassionate enquiry and an empathic witness to my pain, I may have rebuilt trust and been open to receiving love.

However, my experience was very different to this ideal. When my grief surfaced over losses that may have been judged as minor at the time, I would be sent to my room alone to cry. Is that love? It was my parents' inability to contain my grief as well as their own. I don't blame my parents for this, because they hadn't come to terms with their own losses and grief, and they weren't aware of the special needs of their adopted children.

Valerie

Being told that you can't conceive must be devastating. My adoptive mother Valerie was told in a cold and abrupt manner that she would have to accept the fact that she would never be able to have children. At that moment her dreams were crushed and her life irreversibly changed. To a woman who loved children, and whose primary goal in life was to marry and have children, it was a brutal bombshell. She wasn't offered any counselling, comfort or support to grieve. Can you imagine?

Valerie had done babysitting jobs in her local village in England since she was twelve years old. She was in high demand because of her love of babies and children, along with her strong sense of responsibility and competence beyond her years. When Val left school, she studied to become a nurse. During the Second World War she met John, an Irish RAF soldier who had been hospitalised with septicaemia. They started dating, and two years later, when John returned from his deployment in Burma, they were married. They immigrated to Australia in the 1950s.

Val was in her twenties when she worked as a nurse on the paediatric ward of a Sydney hospital, where she sometimes took long-term paediatric patients on outings in her own time. My adoptive mum was the most kindhearted, caring and patient woman I have ever known.

One day, while on duty, she experienced acute pain in her abdomen and had emergency exploratory surgery. When she recovered consciousness, she learned that the surgeon had found gangrene in one of her fallopian tubes, and he had removed both of them in case the infection had spread undetectably. When the ward matron told Val this shocking news, she bluntly said that she needed to accept her lot and carry on.

This was the story my adoptive mother told me, as incredulous as it sounded to me ... that the doctor would render her infertile as a *precaution*. Her unresolved grief was a grey mantle of melancholy that permeated her life and my childhood. She told me that she wished she had become pregnant before marriage, and that if her tragedy had happened later, when IVF was available, she would still have been able to birth her own biological children.

When I was very young, I came across my mother sitting with her elbows on the dining table, head in hands, as she said, 'I wish I could send you all back.' I felt so sad for her, and my heart sank, knowing that I was a disappointing option.

When my friend Tracy, who is also an adoptee, said that we were 'Band-Aid babies', the term rang true for me because it described exactly how I felt. I tried so hard to be the best adopted daughter I could be for my mother and to heal her and make her happy, but I always felt that I wasn't enough, and would never be enough. Sadly, there was an invisible divide between my mother and me, and we couldn't bond or share love and affection because there was so much unsaid and unfelt in that divide.

If losses are not grieved properly, sorrow and pain will pervade so many aspects of future lives and relationships. It took years for me to fully grieve the loss of my partner Joe and simultaneously the loss of my birth mother, and only when I had emptied my tears could I move forward with a feeling of newness, like a rebirth.

The multi-layered losses inherent in adoption must not be underestimated or overlooked, because disenfranchised grief can act like a slow poison, causing sustained suffering.

9

Disenfranchised Grief

'The loss for the adoptee is unlike other losses we have come to expect in a lifetime, such as death and divorce. Adoption loss is more pervasive, less socially recognised, and more profound.'

—DM Brodinsky and MD Schechter

If grief is expressed, it will lessen in intensity and subside over time. Disenfranchised grief is grief that a person experiences when they suffer a loss that is not openly acknowledged, socially sanctioned or publically mourned. Where disenfranchised grief persists for a long time, it can cause depression, isolation, poor self-esteem and psychosomatic illnesses. People living with disenfranchised grief often have trouble coping with subsequent losses, are likely to have difficulty maintaining healthy relationships, and have a propensity for substance abuse.

My adoptive mother carried unresolved grief and suffered depression over her inability to have her own biological children. Those poignant words 'I wonder what my own daughter would have been like' were permanently imprinted on my mind. I couldn't replace her imaginary daughter. Her grief undermined my relationship with her and, sadly, we were never close. I can't remember ever hugging her when I was a child, and even when I was an adult and tried to hug her, she was very stiff and avoidant.

Val did try her best to be my mother, and demonstrated her caring and kindness through cooking and knitting, and bringing me treats when I was home from school because I was sick (or faking it). She was a good mother in all that she did for me, and my adopted brothers, but when my grief surfaced she couldn't cope and she would send me to my room, sometimes in the terrifying darkness. I was told that I couldn't come out until I stopped crying. My mother punished me for doing what she hadn't done or couldn't do, which was to let out her own sadness. Unexpressed grief creates a barrier to love.

For a great many adoptees, disenfranchised grief is deeply embedded in their bodies, sapping their vitality. Their grief is a solitary burden. Carrying grief in isolation is a most lonely and painful experience. Without acknowledgment, kindness, compassion or community support, grief can become a seeping undercurrent in people's lives, diminishing their potential to experience excitement, happiness and joy.

Suppressing emotions increases the power and influence of those disowned emotions. Over time, withheld anger becomes rage, and according to Gabor Maté, can contribute to autoimmune illness. Repressed sadness becomes a disease of depression.

In his book, *Adoptees Come of Age*, pastoral counsellor Ronald Nydam writes: 'Without the support of the adoptive parents the adoptee is unable to grieve their loss ... Whatever the children's pain might be, we need to be present with them in such a fashion that they learn that their emotions are acceptable.'

Few adoptees, or adoptive or birth mothers, received this kind of emotional support.

Many times throughout my childhood, events would trigger my deep sorrow. I remember when my adoptive father killed a mouse after it ran into the floor polisher to hide. He turned on the polisher to squash it. It was a horribly cruel act, and I was heartbroken. Another time I was in the car when he ran over a cat. When I looked back and saw it writhing around on the road, I begged him to stop, but he drove on.

Whenever I was in distress, I would be sent to my room, where I would curl up into a foetal ball and sob so hard that my body hurt. I will always remember the unbearable loneliness of those times, when I felt utterly unloved.

I look back at myself as a little girl with a heart full of compassion, knowing how different her life could have been had she felt safe and nurtured by the steady support of an adult. Instead, disenfranchised grief affected everything she did, preventing her from being a carefree and joyful child.

Ronald Nydam admits that 'although clinically trained, I, like the American culture of which I am a part, did not understand that relinquishment [the primal wound that may even be prenatal] and adoption ... could have such a profound effect on the development of a person'. He is referring here to a client, Tom, who had presented with marital problems, but as time went on it became clear that

Tom had unresolved grief. 'I slowly learned that Tom had never grieved his relinquishment, which had occurred forty-two years ago ... in his life, he had stretched as far as he could without grieving until he could no longer walk forward in life.'

The effects of birth trauma and disenfranchised grief can lie dormant throughout a person's life until another loss exhumes the pain associated with the original loss.

A 50-year-old adoptee told me that a sudden end to a short-term relationship was the catalyst that unravelled him emotionally over the following year. All the losses in his life, going right back to his birth mother, came to consciousness to be grieved. During a ritual at a residential self-development course, he was able to let go of the past and set himself free to be the person that he really was, that he had been holding undercover for all these years.

A similar unearthing happened to another male adoptee, who'd had a serious accident that had caused the loss of his job, and his marriage. He attended counselling, which revealed his 'primal wound' underneath the layers of his present painful circumstances, and he was supported in grieving the original loss of his mother.

It's very difficult for adoptees to do the core work of grieving because it is hidden grief, and so many adoptees (and I was one) don't think there is any grief. This is because we can't remember the traumatic event. It happened at a pre-verbal time beyond conscious awareness and the memory is encoded in the body.

As Nancy Verrier writes in her book, *The Primal Wound*, 'the unavailability of conscious recall of the event by the victims themselves has contributed to many of the misconceptions about relinquishment and adoption'.

The magnitude of the wound of mother-infant separation through adoption or surrogacy needs to be fully understood and respected. I appreciate that it is an inconvenient truth for people who prefer to believe in the superficial fairy tale that if you take a baby away from their mother at birth and love, and give all that you have to that infant, it is a happy-ever-after heavenly blend. The reality is that the infant has experienced life-changing loss, a loss that equates to a death, and throughout their life they will need to grieve in their own way and in their own time, and with the appropriate support.

This will be a confronting fact for many prospective parents. For those who are brave enough to accept this reality, there are some important questions that still need to be considered. Are they prepared to understand and support the special issues and needs of the child? Are they willing to do the work necessary to build connection and bonding with their child? Can they let the child have their feelings, and can they stay steady? How big is their love? Have they considered fostering? There are tens of thousands of children in Australia who need a safe, stable and loving family environment for a few months, years, or for the rest of their lives through open adoption.

I know how painful it is to see the child you love go through the grieving process. I had to witness and be a solid support for my seven-year-old daughter when her father died. She lay sobbing in my arms and told me it was the worst day of her life. I saw her collapse on the floor and wail in pain for an hour when her beloved cat died a few years later. I knew that she was also releasing more grief over the loss of her dad. I had to put my own pain aside to be there for her. It was hard, but this is what potential parents must know and be prepared for if they are going to take on an infant who has been separated from their mother and family.

It's so much easier to believe the naïve message of adoption and surrogacy, which states that all a child needs is love. Whenever I hear the politically correct slogan, 'Love is love', I want to say that it's not that simple. Yes, it's true that a child needs love, but love in action is being fully present to that child's specific needs.

Love truly is a selfless act of giving without expectation. Love is not perfect, and it's not always happy. Sometimes it's uncomfortable and sometimes it hurts. To love is to be willing to allow another person the time and space to feel their feelings and to be who they are. It's not love to mould a child to be your extension or accessory, or to treat a child as a product to be bought and sold. Children deserve the very best start in life, and it's the responsibility of every one of us to love and nurture them and their connection to their authentic selves.

Above all, we need to respect the powerful and primal mother-child relationship. Adoption loss and grief has too often been obscured by a multitude of contradictory and confusing messages. Abandonment trauma, and associated grief is so deeply hidden that it can be difficult to link to. However, it's important to know that it's there, in the body. With this knowledge, and with the right support from an adoption-informed therapist, adoptee support group, or empathic witness, feelings can be found and expressed in a safe and healthy way.

Facing the fire

Living with repressed emotions is unhealthy. Finding channels for emotional energy is enormously important. The root of the word 'emote' is the Latin word *emovere*, which means to move out or remove. Moving anger out in a conscious way is revitalising and restorative.

At a pivotal time in my life, in my early thirties, I read the brilliant book, *Facing the Fire: Experiencing and Expressing Anger Appropriately*, by John Lee and William Stott. The authors' main message is that rather than rationalising away anger, it should be expressed in a safe way. The authors make a delineation between old, stored (in our cells) anger and present, righteous anger, and say that the former can make us physically ill if we don't clear it out of our psyche and body.

I spent about a year following the guidance and exercises from *Facing the Fire*. One thing I did was to put a cricket bat and an old futon in the spare room. When I got a headache, which often happened after a phone call with my controlling narcissistic ex, or whenever I felt angry or frustrated, I would take the bat and belt that futon with full ferocity until I felt done.

During this process, what usually transpired was that the present circumstance that had fired me up would morph into memories of past injustices and cruelties, usually at the hands of my adoptive father, and possibly further back to the circumstances of my birth. The original feelings of helplessness and rage would rise up and be expelled with each satisfying thwack of that bat. It was so liberating and empowering. My headache would be gone and I'd feel relieved and revived. All the long-standing stored-away anger that I had repressed lifted off me that year. I now express anger appropriately in the present so that it's no longer filed away and festering, and poisoning my relationships. Thank you, John Lee and William Stott.

Righteous anger is a clearer, more present and powerful expression. An example of righteous anger comes from that time when I was following the guidance from *Facing the Fire*. I lived close to the beach, and one morning on my regular run I found the beach littered with all sorts of rubbish, from flares to shampoo bottles, plastic bait bags and fishing line. I went back later with bags and collected a load of refuse. I was incensed by the irresponsibility of fishermen and ships' crews for dumping their rubbish on 'my' beautiful beach.

As I was committed to releasing my anger, I was about to do my usual bat-belting exercise when I had another idea. I called the local newspaper and told them about the state of the beach. A journalist came out and photographed me with my angry face, holding my bags full of rubbish. He did a half-page story with the headline 'Angry resident speaks out about polluted beach'.

Another time, again on the beach, I saw a man punch his dog. I marched over to him and punched him back, figuratively speaking, with my booming verbal tirade. I asked him what he thought he was doing, and why. His pathetic defence upped my anti and he copped a powerful lesson in how to treat a dog. There was a group of people watching from the sidelines who clapped when I'd finished. Righteous anger can shake things up and bring awareness to the need for change. I think there needs to be more of it. I learned that the power of righteous anger can be a transformative force.

Righteous anger comes from a sense of injustice. There are so many injustices in this world, and adoptees have lived experience of extreme injustice—no wonder so many of us are acutely aware of unfairness, disrespect and inequality.

I see many angry adoptees with a righteous sense of injustice and anger regarding their adoption, but when anger is misdirected it can wreak havoc. Anger and rage turned inward is detrimental to our health and wellbeing, and old anger turned outward is a destructive force in relationships.

If you are an adoptee whose life is affected by unexpressed or inappropriately expressed anger, I encourage you to find ways to safely vent and integrate those feelings, either through working with someone or, as I did, via a self-help regime of dedicating physical activity to exorcising anger. Or convert your anger into a passionate drive for positive change in your chosen cause.

10

Misfits and Fringe Dwellers

'Obscuring the true identity of a person leaves her anonymous and unattached, no matter how many names she may acquire. There is a profound psychological isolation in being unrelated to any other person who has ever lived and to be a stranger who never belongs wherever she may be. The anonymous child has no point of reference to identify with or against. She is, as one adoptee said, "always out of context".'

—The Adoption Triangle, A Sorosky,
R Pannor and A Baran

Trying to fit a square peg into a round hole describes what many adoptees feel, not only while growing up within their adoptive family, but in life in general. It's a sense of being an outsider, diminished and different, and not fully engaged or belonging.

Even as a young child I would observe my adoptive family members and think to myself, *Who are these people? They are so different to me.*

When I searched for some semblance to any of them, I couldn't find anything. To describe my feeling of being 'out of context', I think of a cuckoo bird that has no original abode and is placed in an ill-fitting nest, replacing the parent bird's natural offspring.

I was an outsider who didn't belong in either my adoptive family or within the human family as a whole. I only felt calm and connected when I was in nature, or when I was with animals. I regularly rescued stray or injured animals, as I identified with their suffering and need for help. Their unconditional love was such a comfort to me in my lonely world. I used to say that I loved animals more than people. Around people I felt awkward, but with animals I always felt at ease.

In my adoptive family, I portrayed the child that I thought I should be, the one my parents wanted. Instead of feeling relaxed and confident, I was nervously monitoring my surroundings and trying to blend in. I felt like a flawed fake and if I didn't stay on high alert someone, at some time, would see through my disguise.

This fear was vividly played out in a recurring dream I had for years. In the dream I hid behind furniture inside our home as three children walked down the driveway toward the front door. These children were clones of my two adopted brothers and myself, but they were the 'real' children and we were impostors. I would wake from this nightmare in total terror.

When mentioning adoption to non-adopted people, I have observed an interesting reaction. Their eyes kind of glaze over, and it's as though I've just spoken another language. At that point I lose my voice. In that moment it feels yet again like I'm a faded fringe dweller futilely calling from a distant diaspora. In the awkward silence that follows, I hear my inner voice: Why did you have to bring that up? You've over-shared, again.

I used to feel as though I existed in an isolated bubble with a permeable skin, but nonetheless separated from real life by an imperceptible membrane. Unsure of how, where or when to participate, feeling like an imposter, an unconnected oddity—this was my overriding uncomfortable reality. The one-foot-in-and-one-foot-out straddle is an edgy dance. My sense of dwelling on the fringes of normal society, friendship circles, parties, or in any bonded groups, made me deeply sad and lonely.

As a child, I related to the story of the ugly duckling standing out amongst a raft of ducks.

I wanted and wished for an escape from the family of strangers I lived with, and to find my people.

When I was a kid, our family used to drive onto Aldinga Beach with all our clobber and set up camp for much of the day. I would take the little canoe and paddle out about two or three hundred metres offshore, throw out the anchor, and sit there and soak up the solitude. It was so peaceful. I loved being away from my unhappy adoptive family.

There's a reassuring solace in being alone. Letting go of the vigilance and discomfort associated with social situations. With so many triggers in relationships, retreating to the safety of solitude can bring a sigh of relief and relaxation, but it can also coincide with a familiar sense of sad loneliness.

Safety, trust and security are big issues in relationships for adoptees. Relationships can be very challenging for many people, but the challenges are multiplied and magnified for many adoptees. The spectre of abandonment and loss can lurk behind a word our partner utters, an action or inaction. I used to feel that I didn't have enough substance to fully participate in relationships, and in the wider world, with confidence and power.

I would compare myself with my non-adopted friends, who possessed a subtle self-assuredness that was elusive to me. They inhabited their space; when they spoke they assumed they would be listened to; they seemed to have a solid sense of identity and a definite presence. I imagined it had something to do with knowing their histories, and their place within a biological family system, having strong underpinnings in their foundation.

It would be slightly or seriously derailing for me to be present at someone else's family occasion. My former husband, Joe, was one of seven children, and his large extended family would all gather at Christmas. I can remember having to go for a solo walk to cry and ease my anxiety and wretched sense of not belonging. Even though the family embraced me, I still felt the lack of my own family history, culture and connection. Betwixt and between, neither here nor there, on the outside looking in, ambiguous and alone: this was my silent secret.

I used to feel so flawed that I was constantly looking for new ways to fix myself. A new modality, self-help retreat or personal-development course would hopefully make me a better person, a person who would be acceptable to me or (more specifically) acceptable to my inner critic, who told me mercilessly that I wasn't good enough.

In this Covid-19 world, there's a lot of talk about the 'new normal'. Well, adoptees had to adapt to a new normal since the day they became disrupted by adoption. The word 'adaptee' more aptly describes the personality that was shaped by the traumas and losses suffered in early childhood.

Accepting that I carry scars that may at times and to varying degrees be painfully pressured is part of my coming to terms with my reality and myself. Acceptance is a liberating non-judgmental sense of knowing *It just is*, and *I am me* beyond my life circumstances and my post-trauma persona.

It has been wonderful to see the great strides that have been made in accepting and respecting former fringe dwellers such as the LGBTQIA+ community, and victims of gender inequality and child abuse. Many sectors of our communities, which were formerly shunned or relegated, are gradually being brought into the compassionate fold of a more holistic society, but the adoption community still remains an unfairly quiet voice within the community chorus.

It's over time for adoptees to be equally seen, heard and validated for the human rights injustices perpetrated by forced adoption, the intergenerational trauma we have experienced, and our unique world view and wisdom forged from life on the fringe.

Connection and belonging

I recall an instance of being triggered into a sense of not belonging. It happened at an end-of-year school celebration. I suddenly had a weird, surreal feeling of being completely out of place, as though I was utterly abnormal among a crowd of normal people. I looked around me at the school community and felt like a foreigner in a strange country. I felt like I was in a dream. *Who are these people? They aren't my kind of people. What am I doing here? I'm in the wrong place.* My anxiety rose dramatically and I became very distressed. I couldn't hold back the tears as I made a beeline for the door and cried all the way home.

After this incident, as I have often done over the years, I picked up a pen and wrote in my journal. 'No love, no support, alone, lonely, don't belong, misfit, no one sees me, invisible, detached, floating—these are the feelings associated with my condition, still gripping me in the present, still just as painful. I have to accept that I have an invisible illness with no name, but it's chronic and agonising nonetheless. Throughout my life I haven't even known I was sick. I've never been diagnosed. It's a sickness that has not only seriously affected my life, but also people close to me.'

With hindsight, I see that the above school episode resembled my persistent sense of separateness within my adoptive family. Whenever I've been emotionally hijacked by PATSD and the particular anxiety of not belonging, I've wanted to *move*. The tension of being somewhere and feeling as though I was in the wrong place was very difficult to maintain, and the urge to get up and go was overpowering. But the reality of moving from place to place and relationship to relationship never solved the problem. In fact, it exacerbated it.

Throughout my childhood I lived with the anguish of not belonging, and of not being able to tell anyone. It was my agonising secret. My bedroom was my haven and my prison. I felt safe in there. I would stare at myself in the mirror and wonder who that girl really was.

My room gave me some sense of boundary and safety, but I also experienced aching isolation in there. I felt no connection to any other human being.

The search for connection to place and people was a driving force throughout my life until I discovered that reconnecting to *me* was of primary importance.

Comings and goings

Arrivals and departures have always been somewhat problematic for me. As my therapist graciously put it, it's one of my 'sensitivities'. Comings and goings summon up varying degrees of anxiety, stress and sadness in me. When I was a child I regularly suffered with carsickness. I'll never forget that awful queasy feeling and trying so hard not to vomit. I was sick with anxiety. I was also in fear of my tyrant of an adoptive father, and I hated being stuck in the car with him.

Leaving behind the safety and familiarity of home, and sometimes leaving pets behind, was extremely stressful. Even now I can feel anxious and distressed when I have to say goodbye to my kids and pets, even if it's only for a short time.

Feeling connected and then disconnected has been a theme throughout my life. Not surprisingly, I've had boyfriends who are avoidant types, where distance is their way of not being too close and intimate. So getting involved with long-distance, part-time, emotionally unavailable men has been the perfect provocation for my PATSD.

I remember a day when Joe was at work and I tried in vain to contact him for a few hours, by phone and two-way radio. I panicked. My internal alarm system was screaming. Or when I wasn't able to contact my adult daughter and worriedly called several of her friends, much to her embarrassment. In these and many instances I've been absolutely frantic, and catastrophising if I haven't been able to make contact with a loved one.

I once arrived at a venue for a weekend relationship-skills retreat that I'd enrolled in and paid handsomely for. When one of the facilitators opened the front door, rather than warmly welcoming me, she was distracted by someone inside and left me hanging. I just turned around and left. Welcomes have always been very important to me, and because of my sensitivity I always make sure that I invite people into my own home with a hearty welcome. It's important to me that people feel safe and relaxed; an example of getting good at giving what I didn't get.

Warmth and welcome were certainly absent on my arrival into this world. When I witness a newborn being cradled by a loving mother and father, and surrounded by smiling family members and friends, I'm acutely aware of the vastly different experience of separated babies. We were an illegitimate outcome of a sinful union, shunned by society and hidden away in the most unwelcome arrival possible.

Therapy helped me to have compassionate understanding for the part of me that was dislocated at birth. In the past I was told that I was too sensitive, which I would take on board, but I've learned that sensitivity is not a dirty word. Sensitivity is in fact a superpower that lets us know when something isn't right. Many adoptees have a top-of-the-range bullshit detector.

My wonderful therapist also reaffirmed for me that my reactions were ordinary responses to what were extraordinary events in my life. It makes sense that an infant who suffered the calamity of displacement at birth could become an adult who is hypersensitive to comings and goings.

11

Implicit and Explicit Memory

> 'No matter how much insight and understanding we develop, the rational brain is basically impotent to talk the emotional brain out of its own reality.'
>
> —Bessel van der Kolk

Adoptees over the years have shared remarkable stories of events in their lives that have activated a regression to their original trauma, where powerful and often-overwhelming feelings have spontaneously emerged. There is research-based evidence explaining why this occurs. Scientific studies of brain and neurological development reveal that stresses imposed on a growing child during the critical phase from foetus to around age three are recorded and imprinted within the brain's circuitry. A child's early experiences are physically encoded, forming a basic program, much like a hard drive on a computer.

Explicit memory can be recalled, but doesn't develop until approximately age three. Before that, childhood experiences are implicit.

Implicit memory is beyond words, it is an imprint that is held not only in the body, but also in our subconscious habits, gestures and movements. When an implicit memory is activated in the present, it doesn't feel like it's a past memory, it actually feels like the original situation is happening now.

Understanding the meaning of implicit and explicit memory is key for adoptees.

It helps to make sense of some of our unintentional and mystifying reactions. I had spent many years participating in a myriad of self-help groups, therapies and healing modalities, and yet I still had reactions that I seemed to have no control over. Learning about implicit memory explained why.

For example, one day as I was walking through a city park on my own, I must have had a thought that suddenly set me off into a panic attack. I became frozen with anxiety and couldn't walk forward, so I sat down and called my therapist. By a miracle she was available, and she talked me through the episode, starting with a grounding exercise that involved removing my shoes and standing on the grass while she guided my breathing and I calmed down.

Dr Gabor Maté explains that implicit memory only remembers feelings. Dr Arthur Janov, in his book *Primal Healing*, writes: 'When trauma happens early in life, the nervous system is not fully developed, and it can only process a limited amount of stress before there is an overload of pain. That overload is not ignored by the body's system; instead, it is put in storage in the brain neurochemically and is held as imprinted memory. Later, that imprinted memory may give rise to behaviour that reflects a self-image of,

"They don't care about me. What's wrong with me?" It becomes, in the current psychological vernacular, a lack of self-esteem. At its worst, imprinted memory may give rise to depression, anxiety, or high blood pressure, as well as any number of various mental and physical maladies.'

Adoptee separation trauma was laid down in our implicit/cellular memory. We have no recollection of that shocking event. But our body does. Implicit memory is invisible, so we are not even aware that an implicit memory has been activated. This is why adoptees can experience strong reactions and behave in ways that are baffling to others and ourselves. Understanding that we may be having a post-trauma episode stemming from our implicit memory helps us to have loving compassion for our selves.

Remarkably, implicit memory can also reveal itself in dreams and visions ...

12

Meeting My Mother

'Oh, my mama loves me, she loves me
She get down her knees and hug me
Like she loves me like a rock
She rocks me like the rock of ages and loves me
She love me, love me, love me, love me.'

—'Loves Me Like a Rock', Paul Simon

I still love this song, 'Loves Me Like a Rock'. I used to sing it out loud with gusto. It's interesting to look back at beloved songs and understand why they made such a strong and lasting impression. Another favourite was 'Chirpy Chirpy Cheep Cheep' by Middle of the Road. I used to belt out the lyrics and cry. 'Last night I heard my mama singin' this song, woke up this mornin' and my mama was gone'.

The day my adoptive mother first spoke about my adoption is still clear in my mind. I was only four or five, but I vividly remember the moment when I asked her where I came from. I was standing beside her while she worked at the kitchen sink. She was wearing her green-and-white apron over a floral cotton dress, and I looked up at her from hip height as I asked her the classic existential question. Her reply has been permanently engraved in my mind: 'You came out of another woman's tummy.'

I fell silent, and walked away with those perplexing words ringing in my ears. The information didn't shock me or make me feel sad. I didn't feel anything. But it did open up a vast unknown that made me wonder about my missing mother.

I grew up without ever setting eyes on my first mother. Not even a photograph. I was told nothing about her. I was led to believe that knowing my mother, or indeed anything about her, was unimportant, and that I should appreciate how lucky and special I was to have been chosen. I was simply told that my mother couldn't look after me so she did the best thing she could by giving me away.

Throughout my childhood I felt disconnected and different. All my friends looked like other members of their families, even if it was just the shape of their nose. They belonged, but the mould that had shaped me was a one-off. I longed to see someone who looked like me.

I used to imagine my birth mother standing strong and radiating warmth, with her arms open wide, ready to embrace me. My vision of her was of a bright, caring, independent, empowered woman whom I would admire and want to emulate. This image was the embodiment of all the qualities I wished for and all the love I could ever want. Meeting my mother would alleviate all my suffering.

In the late eighties in South Australia, when legislative reform allowed adoptees access to their original birth certificates, I located my mother, whom I will refer to as D. She lived in country Victoria. I wrote to her, and she agreed to meet me. Three weeks later I was on my way to reunion. I was twenty-nine years old and about to meet the woman of my dreams, the goddess figure of my fantasy, the missing piece of me. She would have a red ribbon tied around her bag, and be waiting in the mall outside Myers in Melbourne. I had travelled alone from Northern New South Wales to spend five hours with her.

On the eve of our reunion, I went out for dinner with a friend to an Asian restaurant, and when we got back to her house I started to feel increasingly unwell. Welts began appearing on my body. I looked in the bathroom mirror and, with horror, saw my face blowing up like a red balloon. My airways were swelling and I was finding it hard to breathe. My friend rushed me to hospital.

I was experiencing an anaphylactic reaction to MSG, something that had never happened before. As I lay in the ward bed, I became aware of the child within me silently crying out for the comfort of my mother. In a strange regressed state, I had dreamlike visions of being in a nursery cot, with grey ghostlike nurses gliding by me. I felt indescribable agony and panic. I desperately wanted some solace. I wanted my mother.

The next afternoon I had to meet D with my face still swollen and one of my eyes partially closed. It seemed cruel and unfair that on such a profoundly important day, I was a deformed version of myself. It was a cool grey day, but I wore my sunglasses to hide my puffy eyes. As I walked towards Myers I had the imaginary picture of my mother in my mind's eye, which I had kept safe like a treasure all the years leading up to this moment.

Suddenly there she was, sitting on a bench seat with her back to me. In a weird trance-like state, I stood there in the crowded mall, incognito, as I feasted my eyes on the woman with the red ribbon. I felt frozen in time. It was surreal. What was taking place for me seemed a world away from normal reality. I wanted to savour each moment.

I stepped forward and spoke her name, and in a second I was swept up into her arms and her tears. 'Will you ever forgive me?' she whispered. *Of course I forgive you.*

After those initial defenceless words, I observed D retreat into the safety of denial. As we sat in a noisy cafeteria, she talked incessantly without making eye contact with me. I felt paralysed as I gazed in awe and listened to the woman in front of me: my long-lost mother, my own flesh and blood.

I didn't speak a word as she talked about herself and all the problems that had permeated her life since my birth. D said that her own mother never forgave her for having a child out of wedlock at age sixteen. She said that she loved her three daughters (whom she had after my birth) who meant the world to her and that they mustn't know about me. She looked past me as she said, 'I'm sorry, you just don't feel like a part of me.'

I felt nothing. I was numb. It was as though I was having an out-of-body experience.

The anticlimax of my meeting was so unexpected after years of building an image of my ideal mother and anticipating our happy-ever-after reunion. I had believed that finding her was the final destination in my journey of recovering my lost self, that in her sweeping embrace I would be healed of all the pain of disconnection I had experienced in my life and I would be whole again.

When I got home I wrote to D, telling her how momentous it had been to meet her. She replied with a cold letter telling me to stay out of her life, that her three (other) daughters and her husband knew nothing about me and she wanted it to stay that way.

Some months after this, I had a crashing breakdown. I had great difficulty functioning day to day for a period of about three months. I had no control over my emotions. I would go through the supermarket checkout or make dinner for my family with tears streaming down my face. Some days I couldn't get out of bed because I was so depressed.

When I felt strong enough, and after speaking with an adoption counsellor at Vanish (Victorian Adoption Network for Information and Self Help), I wrote to my mother again and suggested that we might have some mediation and counselling.

I received a solicitor's letter telling me that my communication had caused D distress and that I should cease all contact.

That was over thirty years ago.

I had secretly expected that finding my mother would be my saving grace. Her all-encompassing love would wipe away all of my unworthiness and heal my broken heart. She had been my beacon in a dark day. However, at the end of the day, meeting my mother was a devastating disappointment. As a young mother myself, my children were the loves of my life who I would do and die for, so it was beyond my comprehension that my mother would reject me—again.

I learned a great deal from that reunion. After meeting D at age twenty-nine, I knew that my life, my wellbeing and my destiny were entirely in my hands. Meeting her had been another milestone in my search for my authentic self.

Reunion reality

Some reunions sustain for the long term, dependent on the openness of both parties to delicately dedicate themselves to the process. In many cases, the wounds of separation trauma are exhumed during reunion and the relationship ends. I've met birth mothers and fathers who've had reunions with their adult offspring and have welcomed them with open arms. They have included them in their lives and families, and been generously supportive, and have then experienced erratic contact or the sudden disappearance of their 'relinquished' (adult) child.

I met a father who had elatedly reunited with his long-lost daughter. They spent time getting to know each other and all was going well. He planned and paid for them to have a fabulous overseas trip so he could show her his favourite places in the world. I was mesmerised by his story, and in awe of his generosity and loving willingness to embrace and include his daughter in his life. But his enthusiasm turned to heart-sinking disappointment when, without warning, his daughter broke off contact very close to their departure time. He lost a lot of money, but he forgave her when she resumed contact sometime down the track. The final scene in this ill-fated story involved the theft of his credit-card details and a considerable sum of money, which happened when his daughter stayed at his home while he was away. He later discovered that his daughter had a drug addiction.

This man was understandably utterly perplexed, angry and deeply hurt. I feel compassion for both of them, and I understand that there is no blame to be laid in this very sad situation. Attachment injuries are the fundamental factors that create havoc in personal lives and in reunions. Though I don't condone such hurtful behaviour, I do comprehend the underlying complexities that contribute to it. Hurt people inadvertently hurt people. Lack of trust, fear, unresolved grief, and a sense of unworthiness are some of the contributors to an adopted person's rejecting and acting-out behaviour. Complex trauma can have a lasting impact and influence on the relationships of adult adoptees, not least in reunion with birth mothers and fathers.

Reunion is an extremely sensitive process and it's easy for either party to accidentally detonate a bomb when walking through such an emotional minefield. Implicit memories are resurrected, and regression to the traumatic time of separation can happen for any or all parties, who may become flooded with feelings associated with their painful past.

Embedded adoption propaganda can also influence the reunion. When I met my birth mother she regurgitated the hackneyed platitude, 'I knew you were going to a good home.' It was assumed. She didn't ask me if that was the case, which it surely wasn't.

It's so important for adoptees to be listened to. If birth mothers and fathers could simply listen (at least initially), and not assume, or try to fix, or talk about their own problems and pain, all parties would benefit greatly. The adopted person would feel rightfully regarded. My meeting with D was full of her telling me her woes and how much she loved her (other) daughters, and then at the end, the brutal dismissal. Thirty years later, I'd love to have another opportunity to tell her a few truths.

As I previously said, it has been part of adoption mythology that adopted children are loved even more than non-adopted children because their adoptive parents waited and saved up all their love for their chosen child. In many cases, this belief is far removed from reality.

I have heard some horror stories about adoptive families. I know a man who was adopted into a family who already had two biological children. He was cruelly scapegoated and regularly punished by being locked up in the garden shed. No wonder this man became drug addicted and was incarcerated for acting out violently. Admirably, he fought for his own recovery and has taken a more positive path in his life.

I remember my infant-school teacher calling me to her desk at the front of the class and telling me that she'd heard I was adopted. 'You're so lucky you were chosen,' she said. 'Most parents just have to accept what they get.' In my mind's eye I saw rows of babies in a hospital nursery and my adoptive mother walking up and down peering at all the little faces, deciding which baby to take home, and then pointing at me, saying, 'I'll have that one please.'

The message, that adoptees should be grateful that they were lucky enough to be chosen, is a shameful example of tribal gaslighting, making it difficult for adoptees to know and trust their reality. My reality was that I did *not* feel lucky. I felt sad, lonely, confused and anxious. Imagine saying to a child whose parent has just died, 'Come on, chin up, it's not that bad. Something better is coming your way.'

The shock, loss and grief that an adopted child experiences is utterly dismissed, and replaced by the absurd and cruel notion that they are *lucky*. Hypocrisy, denial and deception are rife in the adoption system, further compounding the injuries already sustained by adoptees.

I have heard some positive stories of reunion between adoptees and their biological families, but I've heard many more to the contrary. I've had three friends whose babies were 'relinquished', and in each case their adult children suddenly ceased contact soon after reunion.

It's important to have support during reunion since it can be an intensely triggering time. Time spent reading and researching, and ideally attending support groups, can help enormously to inform and fortify all parties leading up to reunion. There are also search and support services available to adoptees, such as Jigsaw, and Post Adoption Resource Centre. If facilitated carefully, reunion has a much better chance of lasting the distance.

13

Inner Reunion

'Examine yourself and understand who you are ... Whoever does not know self, does not know anything. But, whoever knows self, has acquired the knowledge of the universe.'

—BOOK OF THOMAS (GNOSTIC GOSPELS)

The most profound revelation I took away from that fateful day in Melbourne when I met D is that inner reunion is the most important alliance. My identity was stolen at my birth, and I mistakenly thought that I could retrieve it by meeting my mother. It turned out that I had to search within to discover who I really was beyond the tangled mess of adoption that had overlaid and obscured my true identity.

My inner odyssey was a deep dive into the wild and wonderful world of my psyche. As I travelled through my intra-terrestrial terrain, I gradually uncovered and developed a relationship with the real me. Getting to know myself, beyond conditioned messages, and beyond the roles I inhabit in my life, continues to be an ever-expanding discovery. Knowing, accepting and confidently expressing who I am is a long way from lost me, and my adapted self.

Inner reunion involves feeling and expressing our feelings, the good, the bad and the ugly. It includes defining ethics, passions, likes and dislikes, and what's important to us. Distilling the lessons and messages from our lived experiences is another great gift that comes out of inner reunion. Knowing what we stand for, acting in alignment with our values, having integrity, and speaking with clarity and honesty are just some of the wonderful outcomes of reunification.

There is nothing greater or more fulfilling than being our authentic self. I know this because I've experienced the difference between my fear-full adapted self and authentic me. I hated the fake me, the one who had a completely different name from the one I later found on my original birth certificate. I didn't like the name that my adoptive parents gave me. It didn't fit. It never felt like my name, and it made me feel weak. I loathed the man who pretended to be my father, who treated me like a worthless idiot to be tolerated and mistreated. The life I lived with my adoptive parents wasn't *my* life and I knew it, but I had to go along with it.

I despised myself for not being real and telling the truth. I was living with people who weren't my people. Living as pretend me in a pretend family made me feel sick. Layer upon layer of lies was burying me alive. It took arduous effort for me to dig down through the rocks and rubble—years of blood, money, sweat and tears. (I reckon fair compensation would be around five million dollars for forced-adoption abduction and corruption of my life. It's difficult to estimate. Perhaps ten million is a more accurate figure.)

I *can* say my hard work paid off, because I'm much happier with who I am now. I'm proud of me. I know who I am, what I believe, what I know, and what I will and will not tolerate, or allow to be part of my world. I know what's real, and I speak truth. The difference between past and present me is like night and day.

Inner reunion can happen with or without a biological-family reunion. My inner reunion has been the most satisfying work of my life. Adoption hypnosis had made my feelings inaccessible, which caused depression and addiction, but every time I discovered and assembled another fragment of myself, I felt more grounded, solid and strengthened.

Voice Dialogue

Drs Hal and Sidra Stone created Voice Dialogue: a method of untangling, understanding and balancing the complex facets of the personality. We all have a family of inner selves that inhabit our psyche, and by drawing out and listening to the various voices or sub-personalities within us, we discover the dominant forces that are directing our beliefs and behaviours beyond our conscious awareness.

Do we really know who is driving our psychological car? Are we being steered by our instinctive wisdom, or primarily by our trauma-formed coping personality?

The main objective of many of the inner selves that inhabit our psychic system is to protect our vulnerability, keep us safe, and gain love and approval. Like all mammals, we are born totally vulnerable and we must attach to our mothers for our sustenance and development. Our very lives depend upon this.

In the case of adoptees, who are taken too soon from our mothers, we developed survival strategies to deal with our trauma and protect us against further hurt. Our personalities evolved tactics to keep us safe from further abandonment.

Voice Dialogue revealed to me that many of my defensive methods were now outdated and actually working against me in my adult life and relationships, for example, the pleaser part of me that cared more and did more for others than for myself, with the unconscious aim of being accepted and loved, and most importantly, not rejected. My overactive pleaser was leaving me on the sidelines of my own life. I was feeling drained and resentful of my lack of attention to my own wellbeing.

Voice Dialogue also enabled me to reclaim the parts of me that were lost in adoption fog, most importantly my life-changing reunion with my inner child, the essential and authentic me that I became detached from when I was born.

As an adoptee, I had complied with the lucky-and-should-be grateful edict, further disowning my authentic feelings. My intuitive senses had been gaslit and silenced.

Through Voice Dialogue, I reunited with my long-lost authentic feelings. The process also supported me in finetuning the volume of my internal dialogue, turning down the dial on distressing self-defeating thoughts, and increasing the power of my healthy, constructive inner dialogue as I learned to be the conductor of my internal orchestra.

Inner selves

Following are some of some of the dominant inner selves of adopted people.

Inner Critic

> The inner critic can be a heavyweight presence, with great power and persuasion in the psyche of adoptees and anyone who has suffered childhood trauma. Though the critic's intention is to try and make us do better and be better (to be acceptable), we will never be enough if we let this voice run the show. The inner critic can be a debilitating and self-defeating force within us, telling us that we are stupid, useless, or any other putdown in the critic's repertoire.

The Pusher

> An overactive pusher will drive us to do, do, do. The pusher will not stop in the face of fatigue or strain, which is often interpreted as the ability to soldier on or named an overachiever. Unmanaged inner pushers can turn people into workaholics and make them ill through stress if they don't balance this energy. *Doing* all the time is often a way to avoid feeling, maintain control, and feel safe.
>
> I asked a woman whose two sons had been lost to her through adoption why she always knitted quietly and never spoke during our adoption-triangle support-group meetings. She told me, as she continued to

knit, that she made sure to be constantly *doing*, from dawn to falling into bed exhausted. She said it was her way of avoiding thinking about and feeling the loss of her boys.

The Pleaser

Not to be confused with a kind and caring aspect of our personality, the pleaser is super nice and bends over backwards in order to win love and approval from others, and not be rejected. This sub personality will say yes to a request or demand every time! The pleaser does for others at their own expense, which can lead to resentment over time. 'What about me?' is a common refrain from pleasers. Pleasers tend to leave themselves out of the picture of their own lives.

The Rebel

Many adoptees will relate to this sub personality. Anger, defiance and hurt drive the rebel. The rebel has a *fuck-you* attitude to being controlled or curtailed, and typically resists rules and laws. The rebel can be counterproductive and cause trouble (my own rebel got away with a lot of lawlessness, but also caused me some problems). However, when channelled consciously and positively, rebel energy can shake things up and change things for the better.

Police chase

One story from my rebellious, risk-taking past began on an early blue-skyed summer morning. I'll infuse this story with my unashamed attitude at the time ...

I had taken my four dogs down to the beach for our usual run and swim. As I cruised toward home, feeling salty and content, I saw on my side of the road a police breathalyser—at around 8.30 am. They pulled me over and discovered that my registration had recently expired. My fault. I take full responsibility for letting my rego slip. But then I was told that I couldn't drive home. My car was parked on the side of the road, no shade, with four dogs in the back. Heat was rapidly rising—in the air, and in my veins. I hadn't taken my phone with me to the beach so I had no way of calling anyone to my rescue.

I tried reasoning with the cop. I told him that I had friends who lived about a kilometre down the road, where I could leave my car and they would drive me home with my dogs. No, I could call a taxi, said wanker. What taxi would take four dogs? No pleading or reasoning got through his thick head.

At this point my blood was boiling. There was no way I was going to leave my dogs stranded in a hot car. My anxiety was through the roof. My beloved dogs' safety and wellbeing was being threatened, and if any of my loved ones are threatened I will fight, to the death if necessary. And no one will exert senseless control over me.

As the cop walked back to his vehicle, I jumped in my car and took off. I saw in my rearview mirror the two police grab the orange cones from the roadside and get into separate cars.

I was approaching a crossroad and had to think fast. I took a left turn onto the main road, a very quick right turn down a side street, and another left down another street until I found a snug hiding spot close to some trees, adjacent to the main road. I could hear and see one of the police cars screaming along the main road with its siren on; the other car went racing in the other direction.

I sat there for a few minutes before making my move to get back out to the road and head for home. I just needed to get to the safety of home base. After that I didn't care what happened.

I tentatively pulled out onto the main road. All clear. I turned in the direction of home. Crap! One of the police cars was coming toward me, and when the cop saw me, he screeched to a halt, did a sharp U-turn, turned on the siren and tailgated me. I was still determined to get home. I kept driving steadily and calmly, at the speed limit, with the sound of a siren on steroids and the police car so close behind mine that I could see the cop's furious face in my rearview mirror. After a couple of minutes, he stopped chasing me and pulled over.

I carried on a short distance to my friends' house, where I explained my situation. We piled in their car and they drove us to my house, where the police were waiting for me. One porky bloke was visibly red and shaking with rage, and the other was standing there coolly, with a recorder in his hand. He interrogated me and I answered honestly. I kept repeating that I had needed to get my dogs home. They left, and some time later I received a litany of charges and fines, which I paid off over years.

There was a period in my life when I defied authority with the fierceness of a wild woman. If I couldn't make sense of rules, controls and regulations, I would rebel with vengeance. I had no time for stupidity.

In another incident, I swore at two police officers who had pulled me over. They couldn't give me a real and rational response to my question, so I called them 'stupid fuckers' and they threatened to arrest me.

There have been several other altercations that I won't bore you with. Basically, I was operating from a part of me that'd had enough of being taken advantage of, controlled and disrespected. I will say that my inner rebel has since mellowed. I know now that there are smarter ways to fight, and more diplomatic approaches to dealing with power, injustice and ignorance, but the fighter within me is as strong as ever. It's a force to be reckoned with, born of my helplessness at the hands of an unjust adoption scam.

The Independent

In an article called 'Nurturing Attachment', published in the Post Adoption Resource Centre newsletter, clinical social worker Deborah Gray writes that 'anxious people do not know who they can trust to help them. Their "independence" is a false one, meaning that they do not trust others and can only rely on themselves'.

As with all coping selves, there is a positive and negative aspect to them, including the fierce independence I see in many adoptees. Yes, we may have a great ability to endure and soldier on through tough times. And we may be resilient as a result of early trauma. We can hold it together like no one else. These are great strengths, but if we don't know how and when to be vulnerable and reach out to others, then these traits can create problems, especially in forming and maintaining close relationships.

In Marlou Russell's book, *Adoption Wisdom*, she writes: 'The awareness of having survived can give adoptees strength and determination in various areas of their lives. The downside of this feeling of survival is that some adoptees find it difficult to depend on others and instead are very independent. It is important for adoptees to realise that healthy relationships involve interdependence—depending on one's self and depending on others.'

14

Inner Child

*'Hold the hand of the child that lives in your soul.
For this child, nothing is impossible.'*

—Paulo Coelho

Embracing my inner child transformed me from a self-rejecting, semi-real, semi-alive alien to a connected, self-accepting authentic human.

The loss of my self felt like an empty space in my chest. I had a sense of not being fully connected to my body. Like many adoptees, my life became a search for what was missing.

Unknown to me, my inner child was a deeply wounded, isolated part of me. Instead of recognising her, and responding to her anxious cries and calls, she remained well away from my conscious awareness. In Voice Dialogue terminology, she had been 'disowned'. There's no self-blame here, because what happened to me was a fracture so profound that I had no thread of relationship with this essential part of me, my vulnerability.

Normally a baby's connection to mother and to self is nurtured and gently supported as the baby grows. The infant is securely anchored and feels safe and content. To the contrary, the shocking experience of original disconnection is the hurtling astronaut I used to see in my imagination—untethered and lost.

Finding Voice Dialogue was one of the divine keys that appeared in my world. With it, I was able to unlock the dungeon door of my unconscious, where I ultimately found a lost and lonely infant within my psyche who had no connection to my adult self. This was my first experience of my inner child, and I will never forget it. I saw how my inner critic had shunned and dismissed my inner child as a weak and useless part of me, a part that was unproductive and needy and didn't deserve any attention.

When my Voice-Dialogue facilitator first asked me questions about my inner child I just wrote her off with disgust and disdain. I was asked if I could find compassion and kindness—the same compassion and kindness I gave to my children and animals—for this vulnerable and tortured soul within me. Not only did I have no such compassion for my inner child, but also I had no sense of connection to her at all. Not one iota.

But I gradually recognised that my inner child was the part of me that would surface in my world as depression, as repetitive bouts of deep sobbing, and as an ever-present subterranean sorrow. This was the energy of my rejected, disconnected, grieving inner child.

As my facilitator gently encouraged and guided me to approach her, interestingly I could see in my mind's eye a lost infant weeping and wandering in a grey mist. Very slowly, and with sensitive words of support from my fabulous facilitator, I finally took the small hand of my inner child. Holding that hand and reconnecting with my essential self was a very emotional moment. Time stood still as I attached to the part of me that had been detached since my birth. It was a profound healing unification.

In terms of the shamanic practice of soul retrieval, this is what occurred during my Voice-Dialogue journey. From a shamanic perspective, soul loss is a helpful response that removes us from suffering and pain at the time of trauma. In shamanic teaching, it is important to retrieve and re-embody the fragmented parts of our selves within three days—and restore wholeness. If we don't heal this psychic soul injury we will be out of balance, which can cause physical and mental illness.

Soul loss is what happened to me when I was born. All my life I had been searching, but I didn't know what I was searching for. I was searching for *me*. The lost and found treasure was *me*. Since my vital essence has been returned to me, my relationship with myself has grown and my life has continued to flourish.

It is a sad reality that the lack of appropriate treatment for adoptees after our birth trauma has meant that so many of us have struggled with illnesses such as depression or anxiety, or addiction. Many of us have lived with a vague sense of something missing, or insecurity, or difficulties making our way in life or enjoying loving relationships. I cannot overstate the severity of injury caused to an infant removed from their mother.

I believe that this reclamation is central for every human being, and anyone who has suffered a trauma at some stage of their development has the challenge of reclaiming those parts of themselves that were hurt, fragmented or rejected. To feel whole and anchored fully in the body, and to live a soul-centred life is a wonderful renewal.

Adoptees mustn't continue to abandon themselves in the same way they were abandoned at birth. There may be a part of you that desperately needs your own loving attention. For adoptees, finding the fragments of the self that were jettisoned through trauma is the most important reunion: inner reunion.

15

Reclaiming Your Inner Child

> 'Our vulnerability, and the inner child who carries this vulnerability, is the part of us that is closest to our essential being.'
>
> —Hal and Sidra Stone

'There is a sense of emptiness, a feeling of something missing, of not being whole. Who am I beyond the roles I play in life, and the face I show? I am a woman, a mother, a wife, a sister, but who am I?' This is an excerpt from one of my journals during the early years of my search.

Judith Viorst, author of *Necessary Losses*, defines authenticity as 'our truest, strongest, deepest self that persists over time in spite of constant change'. In order to reclaim our authentic self that was lost to us through adoption, we can begin by looking back in time to when we were at our most vulnerable—infancy—to understand what happened to us when we were separated from our mothers.

Since it's not possible to connect directly to the babies we were, adoptees can think objectively about *any* baby.

Here's the picture.

A small baby cries for mother. Mother responds by picking up her baby. She holds the baby close and cuddles her, making soothing sounds. She rocks the baby gently, feeds her and changes her nappy, giving loving comfort to the vulnerable newborn. Satisfied, baby relaxes into a feeling of safety and calm, knowing that when she communicates, she is responded to, and she feels loved, trusting, and secure. The baby has expressed her need and her need has been met.

Pam Cordano, in her book, *10 Foundations for a Meaningful Life*, talks about bonding being the way out of loneliness: bonding = call + response. When we ask for help from someone and they respond kindly to our call, we begin to trust and bond with them.

In contrast, imagine that a baby's cries bring no response. Mother is nowhere in the vicinity. The baby lies alone in a cot in a sterile hospital nursery, where no one gives her personalised attention, only scheduled feeding and nappy changing. Baby hears no soothing sounds, and has no loving arms to hold her and relieve her stress. She is alone in a cold and strange environment, with no sense of connection, contentment or safety.

The baby continues crying, which gradually becomes screaming and, after a time, hysteria. Baby is now totally panicked, but still there is no sign of mother. No amount of crying and screaming, hour after hour, day after day, brings reprieve from her trauma. Mother is gone and is never coming back.

Now consider that this distraught baby was once you. This was what you went through. How do you think you coped with such extreme distress? What messages were encoded in your implicit memory? What did you learn about yourself and the world? What affect did this trauma have on your neurological and hormonal systems?

I find it difficult to comprehend that some babies held in hospital nurseries before their adoption were sedated to stop the sound of their suffering. 'According to some social workers who worked at adoption agencies, this is the stage at which babies were administered Phenobarbital in order to quiet the anguish and rage as they cry for their missing mothers.' Nancy Verrier, author of *The Primal Wound*.

Either under the influence of drugs, or due to the lack of response to their cries, the distressed baby shuts down. After a sustained lack of response to their calls, they learn to stop calling. When their need for physical and emotional reassurance is not met, they learn that their cries have no impact. They learn that close connection to another human is unreliable. They learn that they don't matter.

And so an adoptee's first relationship with their mother comes to an abrupt and terrifying end. They experience a void, with no feedback, no physical mirroring, and no relief from their intense suffering. They are in an acute state of tension.

By the time adoptees are given to their adoptive parents after possibly weeks in a hospital nursery, they have been seriously disturbed by their traumatic first few weeks of life. Their adoptive parents have no awareness of the ordeal their baby has endured, and how it will condition their adopted child's future.

Neglected and traumatised inner infants can have commanding influence over our adult lives. This inner child will sabotage our relationships through anxiety, mistrust, insecurity, anger and inability to maintain connection. When a situation triggers our vulnerability we will regress to our immature self and act out without our conscious knowing. This will hinder our experience of mature love and intimacy. It is essential that we reconnect to our vulnerability and understand that at the core of our issues with intimacy, self-sabotage and suffering is unhealed trauma. These unconscious wounds can have a damaging impact on us, and others within our circle.

An example of an unhinged episode involving my wounded inner child happened when my first son was a baby. My partner and I had moved from our cottage at Sheheree near Killarney in Ireland to a little converted cow bales in a field of black-faced sheep in Muckross. I can't remember what precipitated the incident, but on this particular day my controlling partner locked me outside the house with my baby son inside. Being separated from my baby propelled me into full-blown panic and rage. I found a metal rake and swung the rake steadily, with full force, driving it into the wooden door. I yanked it out of the door and forced it back in each time with such ferocity that I'll never forget the feeling. Killer rage coursed through me as I screamed like a demon and forced my way in.

No one will keep me from my child, not then, not now, not ever. My fierce protection of my children is powered by PATSD.

One of the life-changing books in my library is *Homecoming*, by John Bradshaw, who writes: 'I believe that the neglected, wounded, inner child of the past is the major source of human misery.'

My wounded self used to dominate my life and relationships. Before I recognised and reclaimed her, I would swing like a pendulum on a seesaw of emotional highs and lows. I had very little control over my emotions when my PATSD was activated. Also, my wounded inner child was continually searching for someone to love her (like a replacement mother), and would overattach or reject in an unconscious perpetual replay. I had no relationship to my inner child, and certainly no idea how to look after this vulnerable essence of me.

In the same way that children try to get the attention of neglectful parents by their acting-out behaviours, my inner child would run amok and desperately seek attention through tears, tantrums and tirades. And just as some parents react to their child's attention-seeking actions by chastising them, I would continue to abandon, punish and rewound my inner child with critical, dismissive inner dialogue.

Rather than looking within and giving my self the love and support I needed to heal, I was looking outside for validation and care. Looking for love in all the wrong places would just end up affirming the beliefs I had formed from my early life: that I was bad, flawed, stupid and unlovable.

My internalised abandonment kept showing up in my external world as an outward projection of my unhealed story. (It's interesting that even my own birth mother chose and still chooses to deny reality and ignore my existence.) I had to claim the existence of my self: the part of me that became lost at the moment of my birth. Instead of ignoring her, I needed to find a way to reunite with and embrace my abandoned inner child.

Bonding with, and nurturing a relationship with our inner child is the way of true healing. When we give to ourselves what we needed and didn't receive, we heal and restore our authentic selves, allowing our innate wisdom to become our guiding light.

16

My Devastating Wake-up Call

'By riding the wave of your dark night, you are more yourself, moving toward who you are meant to be.'

—Thomas Moore

B J Lifton, in her book *Lost and Found*, says that she thinks of adoptees as being part of the great tradition of sleepers. 'It is as if the act of adoption put us under a spell that numbed our consciousness. When we awaken it startles us to realise we might have slept our lives away, floating and uprooted.'

Someone once said to me that life keeps presenting us with what we need to learn about ourselves. She used the expression 'pebble, rock, house'. In a metaphorical sense, she meant that if we don't take notice of the pebble that hits us, a rock will fall, and if that doesn't wake us up, a house will descend on us.

The devastation of Joe's death woke me up out of the great adoption sleep.

When Joe died, my old life came to an abrupt end. Before that terrible day I had been sleepwalking through my life, unconsciously driven by the trauma-driven coping behaviours that had been insidiously debilitating me and impeding my relationships for over forty years. I had been carrying a deep attachment wound since birth, and was left undiagnosed and untreated while my wound festered under cover of denial prescribed by the closed-adoption system.

On the day that Joe died I twice had an intuitive prompt to call him and make peace after an argument we'd had. But I didn't because I was too afraid that he would be angry. Back then I couldn't handle it when a man was angry. Any man. I still remember with crystal clarity looking down the hallway at the phone and hearing a whisper over my shoulder telling me to ring him. Instead, I ignored the guidance and the phone sat there like a ticking bomb.

Later that day, the phone rang, exploding with the horrendous news of Joe's death. The force of the shock flattened me to the floor, and in that moment all my defences, constructed since my birth, shattered into a million pieces. At the same time, it was as if a blinding light exposed the dream in which I had been living: the unreality of my post-trauma personality. Everything I thought I knew was cast into oblivion with the agony of losing Joe, my soulmate and my daughter's father.

I was riddled with regret for not making that call; the what-ifs and if-onlys were a maddening mainstay in my mind over the following months. I went over and over my words, actions and inactions, and believed that if I had only made that call Joe would be alive. If only I had talked to him and let him know the truth: that I loved him and was feeling very hurt. If only I had been bold enough to make that call and express my feelings. Every cell of my body ached with the pain of regret. Each morning was Groundhog Day, when I relived the shocking reality that Joe was gone.

I cried every day for nine months (I noted the first day that I didn't cry and later reflected on the coincidence that human gestation is nine months). On one of those days, as I lay in bed in the familiar foetal position, experiencing an avalanche of grief, I became aware that I was simultaneously grieving the loss of my mother and the loss of my partner. Both losses criss-crossed my consciousness as I cried torrents of tears.

When my crying time was over, I felt as though I had emptied out all the repressed sorrow that had been locked up within me for all of my life to that point. I felt light and unburdened for the first time. I still mourned and missed Joe, and still do to this day, but I no longer carry the deep disenfranchised grief that had underlined my life, only surfacing like the tip of an iceberg when I experienced losses such as the death of a pet or a perceived rejection, or even an imagined loss.

Harvill Hendrix and Helen Hunt, in *Receiving Love,* state that the task of becoming conscious can be successfully accomplished by anyone who wants to undertake the effort. Even if you've sleepwalked through all of your relationships up to now, it's not too late to wake up.

It took a monumental impact to wake me up. Joe's sudden death was my dark night of the soul, and a profound part of my recovery and restoration.

Validation salvation

Validation is gold. It's the connecting, calming balm that helps us to feel valued, understood, cared for and worthwhile. Validation makes us feel that our feelings, perspectives, and who we uniquely are, matter. Validation comforts us when we feel heard and understood. Validation really has been my salvation.

In my life, I desperately searched for validation from the outside. To be validated was something I hadn't experienced very much. I wanted my feelings to be affirmed by the people around me, and for them to see my point of view. I would disclose in the hope that people would at least attempt to understand me and validate my feelings when I expressed them. Instead, I was often judged, dismissed, gaslit or ignored.

Echoes of my childhood would reverberate and exhume my secret sadness every time. Painful memories of being invalidated as a child would come flooding into my mind, of being shut in my room in the darkness, screaming, while being told that I wouldn't be let out until I stopped crying. I'll never forget the intensity of my terror and the force of my screams (to this day my involuntary blood-curdling screams can literally send people running for cover).

My adoptive father's specialty was humiliation and a beating whenever I didn't obey his repressive rules that essentially were: do as you're told and what's expected, keep up a perfect façade, and don't rock the boat. I was rejected for being anything other than pleasant, quiet and compliant. Growing up in such a suppressive, invalidating environment diminished me and made me feel worthless. I was so removed from my feelings and perceptions of my reality that I walked through life in a hazy melancholic mist.

I feel fortunate to have had a therapist who provided me with the validation I had missed out on. I have also attended support groups with people who told their stories and communicated their feelings, which was wonderfully validating. Unfortunately, many adoptees haven't had the validation they need and deserve. People generally haven't been taught the importance and skill of validation.

Invalidation includes denying, blaming, judging, minimising or dismissing feelings or experiences. Invalidation says: *I don't care about your feelings. Your feelings are unimportant. Your feelings don't matter. You shouldn't feel that way.*

The adoption process is immensely invalidating to adoptees. We experienced invalidation right at the beginning of our lives, when we were denied the most important human relationship with our mother, the person who nurtured us to life in her body. I can't think of any greater invalidation than that of disregarding a human baby's primal need to be with their mother. In hospital nurseries the unheard, unattended and sometimes suppressed cries and screams of separated newborns were invalidated. Adoptees' learned that their calls and needs didn't matter, were unimportant; many learned that *they* didn't matter.

Adoptees feelings were continuously discounted and overridden by messages that denied the traumatic reality of being taken. There was no validation of the combined losses of a sense of safety, trust and security; connection to family of origin; sense of place, identity and belonging; and, most heinous, loss of self.

Adoptees' authentic birth certificates were invalidated and a new—false—birth certificate issued. The truth about our origins was erased to provide a clean-slate baby to adopters. Abolishing the heredity and identity of an adopted person is an indefensible invalidation. It is every human's birthright to know their ancestry, to know themselves.

And of course many adoptees can relate to the classic invalidating response that is commonly given when we say that we were adopted: we are lucky, we should be grateful. A better approach would be to try to understand by asking questions and listening. Curiosity and genuine interest is wonderfully validating for anyone.

It has taken decades of my life to learn to acknowledge and validate my feelings; to listen to the cries and whispers of my inner child and be the support that I idealised would be provided by others. Part of my process also involved letting go of some people who habitually invalidated me, and as difficult and scary as that has been it has been worthwhile. My therapist was so right when she said that with certain people, when you need some support and lean back there's nothing to lean back on.

Emotional support is an important prerequisite for friendship, and I no longer accept fair-weather friends into my close sphere. It's been liberating to realise that I can choose to be surrounded by people who can truly listen, understand (or try to), validate and encourage. This is one of the defining lessons in my life.

I've learned that self-validation is deeply soothing. Self-validation has made my feelings important—to myself. Self-validation is me saying to myself that it's understandable that I would feel a certain way; that my feelings are valid and I'm here for me, to defend and protect myself if needed. It's me telling myself: *You're okay; I care about you, you matter.*

If I'm upset over something, rather than berate myself or dismiss my feelings, I will compassionately care for that part of me that is hurt, and my inner voice speaks to myself in the same way that I would speak to an upset child—gently, and empathetically, giving affirming and reassuring messages.

When I practised self-validation, I experienced its healing power from within. The quality of my life has improved immeasurably with an inside-out rather than outside-in approach.

Adoptees merit the utmost respect and validation for what they endured at the very start of their lives, and for simply being who they are, just the way they are. We have experienced many losses, and it can be a long and winding path to recover some of those losses. Some will never be recovered. These are the sensitivities we live with. But with growing self-care, kindness and validation, we can be a more positive force in our lives. And the scars that we carry can be our contributions to creating a kinder world.

Unfortunately, the injuries sustained through mother-infant amputation continue to be invalidated by mainstream society.

Gushing celebrity

Whenever I've felt doubt creeping in about the need for this book, I've been reinvigorated with fervour when I hear a sugary surrogate story that excludes the voice and needs of the child at the very centre of the narrative. Surrogacy, like adoption, is still thinly portrayed as a happy-ever-after story.

I once witnessed the saccharin superficiality of a gushing celebrity announcing that he and his husband were 'expecting' (doesn't he mean 'commissioning'?) their third baby.

Nameless celebrity told the quaint story of his son asking whether he came out of his (the celebrity's) tummy, and his reply was that he had borrowed a woman's tummy. Mr Celebrity laughed when he recalled that his son went silent and walked away. His interpretation was that his son was so obviously disinterested in the answer that it was a non-issue, and all that mattered was that his son was loved and cherished by his two daddies. I cringed at the ignorance and dismissal of the child's reality.

To the contrary, there was a lot going on in that little boy's silence. He was too young to comprehend those words and too young to respond verbally, but he was feeling a lot.

I clearly remember how I fell silent after my adoptive mother told me that I came out of another woman's tummy. I felt ill at ease, confused and uncertain. I don't remember verbal thoughts, but the vast unknown that was opened up with those words was a swirling muddle of unreality and discomfort inside me. From my adult viewpoint now, I imagine questions like: *Who was that other woman? Where is she? Why can't I see her? Why did I come out of another woman's tummy?*

Back to Mr Celebrity. He talked about the phone interviews he had done with potential surrogates. He claimed that he chose the woman who impressed him most because she was very spiritual. She told him that there was nothing more wonderful than giving the gift of life. In this I heard distinct echoes of the better-off-going-to-a-good-home mantra.

Both sugar-coatings are missing major ingredients, namely the experience, rights, needs and wellbeing of the child. Oh, and there's the glaring omission of the handsome sum of money paid to the surrogate. Let's be real.

I recently watched Molly Meldrum interview a famous singer, asking her when she was going to become a mother. She was well past her childbearing prime, but he said to her that if Elton John could become a father, anything was possible. She responded, 'There's more than one way to skin a cat.'

I am rendered speechless whenever I witness the flippant attitudes related to procuring children. In these scenarios no one is thinking of the rights of the child. They are only thinking of themselves and *their* right, *their* desire.

It's convenient to believe fairy-tale thinking when you desperately want a baby but can't have one by natural means, or if gestating your baby yourself is inconvenient for you in your busy life, or if you'd rather not ruin your picture-perfect body by producing and pushing out a baby yourself.

People often choose to believe what they want to believe in order to have what they want to have, without confronting any perceived negatives. They don't want to feel pain: the pain of loss or the pain of not having what they want. They don't want the pain that is invariably part of life, or they have a sense of entitlement, believing that they have the right to something. If someone else has something, then so should they.

But a baby is not the same as a fridge, or a pool, or any other commodity that can be bought and sold. Procuring a child should not be at the expense of that child's health and wellbeing. I know it's an unpopular suggestion in this era but there are some times when we need to face and accept the loss and grief of not having what we want.

To me it's staggering to know that it's now possible to order a gene-based, embryo-selected designer baby that is advertised like any supermarket product. *Announcing eye-colour selection now! Guarantee the sex of your baby! Do you want a lighter or darker skinned baby? You can even choose your preferred delivery date and astrological sign!* Excuse me while I throw up. Children are not products to be tailored to our desire.

In the United States, prospective adoptive parents can negotiate to acquire a baby directly from expectant mothers via Craigslist ads. People who adopt children, often from overseas, and then change their minds can find new homes for those children on Facebook adoption-disruption groups, without any supervision from child welfare agencies (https://www.wired.com/story/adoption-moved-to-facebook-and-a-war-began/).

Child trafficking by way of commercial surrogacy is a burgeoning industry. What has happened to our moral compass? How far removed from nature are we willing to go? What effect will this detachment have on individuals, our society and our planet?

In my opinion, the most blatant anti-nature act is to snatch a baby from the womb. A man taking off his shirt and putting the baby against his chest in order to 'bond' (as another famous male couple shared in an interview) is tantamount to putting a Band-Aid on a deep wound. Nothing and no one compares to the birth mother, whom the baby is intimately connected to. And the woman who gives birth to the baby is the mother; the *surrogate* is the mother.

The innate longing for biological connection is instinctual. Deliberately breaking a child's ties to their organic origins is heinous. Children's rights and needs should take precedence over adult desires. If babies are to be given the best start in life, the mother-child bond and family connection should be preserved unless there are exceptional circumstances. An unstressed, bonded baby becomes a secure child, and a secure child is in a much stronger position to navigate life confidently.

17

Love Your Self

'Love heals the wound it makes.'

—Eva Cassidy

Imagine a society where all infants are welcomed into the world with consistent loving support. They stay safe, steady and connected to their mother, father, extended family, their ancestry, and to themselves as they develop. They have their needs attended to, and hear positive messages of validation, acceptance, and encouragement.

We all deserve this level of love. If we received it, we would love and care for ourselves, each other and our living planet. What a world it would be. Inner peace would become world peace.

The crappy reality is that most of us haven't had this kind of streamlined star-studded childhood. Even crappier that it's now up to us to fill the deficit. I, like many adoptees, had formed a core belief that I was bad and unworthy, so self-love was a way-out concept to me.

I used to feel annoyed and confused every time I heard someone say, 'You need to love yourself.' Whenever anyone said those words to me I would silently tell them to fuck off. I really couldn't comprehend what it meant to 'love yourself'.

After years of rejecting this over-used, abstract new-age 'truism', I gradually came to understand what self-love means. For much of my life I had searched for what I had missed out on: someone to love me unconditionally. After years of striving to find this love (in all the wrong places) my hard-fought-for revelation was that the successful strategy was to—wait for it—love myself unconditionally.

Many adoptees I've met have been sensitive and empathic—carers and rescuers, fighters for the underdog and for justice. Compassionate understanding for others often comes from having suffered, which makes people sensitive to another's pain. Empathy is the gold of adversity. But adoptees need to be careful not to allow their caring for others to override their attention to their own wellbeing.

My tendency was always to give more to others than myself. I gave and supported with the ambition of making others feel loved and happy. I still want to help others now, but in the past I would do so at my own expense. I really had no idea about how to make *myself* the focus of my caring. When I was working as a masseuse in a health retreat, one of my clients presented me with a book at the end of her stay, titled *When I Loved Myself Enough*. I remember wondering why she had given it to me. What was she seeing in me? The beautiful intuitive young woman was Miranda Kerr, who has since spread the message of self-care through her books and beauty products.

It's been a long road of recovery and restoration of myself, and the most important lesson I've learned is to accept and love myself. I didn't have to change my strengths and qualities, such as empathy and concern for others, but what I needed to do was amp up my self-care and compassion. It was like balancing the volume of the part of myself that was so good at giving to others and redirecting a fair share of it to me.

'We get good at giving what we didn't get.' I don't remember where I heard this tongue twister, but I thought it was spot on. Let's get gooder at giving what we didn't get—to ourselves. Loving ourselves means being kind, looking at and speaking to ourselves with soft eyes and gentle words. Forgiving ourselves for making mistakes and moving on, having learned valuable lessons. We must stop punishing and criticising ourselves for past mistakes or false beliefs. What stands between us and more love in our lives is most likely us.

It was a difficult pill for me to swallow, the one that contained self-love. Thinking highly of myself was not part of my childhood programming.

Self-love is the way forward into the life we are meant to live, a life where we shine.

When we take responsibility for investing love and attention in ourselves, everything in life starts to change for the better. Hearing our inner voice that's telling us about our desires, concerns and needs, and responding to them, is deeply satisfying. The call-and-response bonding experience that we missed out on in early childhood is replicated in our self-care experience. Our love heals the wounds we've carried.

The Buddha said, 'You, yourself, as much as anybody in the entire universe, deserve your love and affection.'

What would love say?

You are amazing. You are strong. You are loved. You are safe. You are worthy. I know you can do it. It's okay that you made a mistake, you'll know better next time. Love would speak words in a tone that is tender and forgiving.

If we spoke to ourselves the way we would speak to a small child or a beloved pet, we would feel a whole lot better. Words that are compassionate, considerate, and accepting convey the message that no matter what has happened to us, whatever mistakes we have committed and regret, and whatever our quirks, shape, colour, weight or appearance, we are distinctly and unapologetically our unique selves. We are like precious diamonds, and our value is priceless. Our facets shine with our own characteristic light, and we are all individual sparks of the one light. All equal and worthy of love and kindness.

Nothing and no one can invalidate this truth, and if we've been told any different, we need to break the shonky contract we signed up to. In the legal profession, the terms of a contract become null and void if false information has been given.

I ditched the adoption contract because it was riddled with lies. *My mother loved me so much that she gave me away. I was lucky to be chosen. I had gone to a better life and should be grateful. My adoptive family was no different to a blood-related family. The loss of my mother at birth was insignificant. Knowing anything about my heritage was unimportant.*

These are just a few. The lies I was told became lies that I told myself. My feelings weren't important or valid. There was something wrong with me. I was less than.

My internal messages become reinforced by the experiences I had and the people I attracted. My forte was falling for narcissistic men, like my father, who dismissed, invalidated and gaslit me, just like the adoption system did to mothers and babies.

What goes around comes around. We reap what we sow. If we have seeds of disrespect, self-criticism and fear sewn into our developing psyche, and if we continue to water those seeds, we will see the fruits of our investment. We will see more criticism, greater fear and continuous self-loathing.

I love plants; I love planting them, and reviving them when I see they're wilting from lack of care. Bringing sick plants back to health has been a favourite pastime and pleasure in my life. I've come to see this as an analogy of my own restoration. When we nourish ourselves with kindness and love, we grow healthier and happier. It's as simple as that.

18

Bold Is Beautiful

'Love, like fortune, favours the bold.'

—EA Bucchianeri

The hero's journey begins with a call to action. It's a call to move out of our comfort zone. Whether we respond to the call is up to us. After all, it's a bold move to take a leap of faith and enter the unknown. It takes courage to face our fears and commit to sorting out our stuff. Peeling away the layers of our conditioning to reveal the truth of who we are can be scary. It can be painful and it can involve loss—loss of the known, and perhaps the loss of people from our lives who have come to expect us to be a certain way.

Change invariably involves uncertainty and some degree of fear. Being bold and opening ourselves to more love and joy can be very scary for adoptees, because if we do we may also let in rejection, loss, and hurt. There are a lot of layers of armour around many adoptee hearts. Remaining closed and protected can be a familiar place for adoptees to dwell, yet living in this safe place reduces opportunities to let in and broaden our experience of life and love.

Bold action. Taking chances. Speaking up. Reaching out. Boldness is expansive. It requires faith and confidence, commitment and determination. Being bold enough to express originality and speak from the heart is enlivening. Dorothea Brande said, 'Act boldly and unseen forces will come to your aid.' Every time I've stepped into the unknown I've felt the unseen support that Dorothea speaks of.

I have always remembered the famous line from *Star Trek*: 'To boldly go where no man has gone before.' I used to feel a surge of exhilaration whenever I heard it; I was excited about the new discoveries that awaited the *Starship Enterprise*. I think I've absorbed that declaration as an underlying omnipresent inspiration. (It made me happy to see William Shatner actually journey into space on Jeff Bezos' Blue Origin rocket.)

Joe Scott was the boldest person I've ever known. He was a larger-than-life character whose enthusiasm, positivity and laughter were infectious. Courage and confidence were synonymous with Joe, and he was a positive dynamo who steered a straight course to achieving his dreams. Teaching people to fly, and taking people on aerial adventures was his passion and purpose, and he built a thriving business based on his ambition to make a living doing what he loved. Here is one of many examples of Joe being bold.

It was a beautiful day and I asked Joe to take me up for a quick spin in the trike, a motorised three-wheeled, two-seater open capsule under a hang-glider wing. Imagine a flying motorbike.

When we got airborne he asked me, 'Where do you want to go?'

'Stradbroke Island would be nice,' I said, half-jokingly.

I thought he'd laugh and suggest somewhere a bit closer, but I should have known better because Joe rarely, if ever, said no to an adventure. So we turned around and landed back at the hangar, packed the camping gear in the trike pod, and up, up, and away we went.

We cruised past the Gold Coast and kept going until we reached South Stradbroke. We had been punching a headwind, which could be why we were low on fuel as we approached the stretch of ocean between South and North Stradbroke.

We looked for somewhere to land, but there was bush below us, and hardly any beach because the tide was up. Approaching the water, Joe said that we could turn around and radio for clearance to land at the Gold Coast Airport or we could 'gun it'.

We gunned it.

North Stradbroke beach was in sight, and as we flew down to land it became obvious that there'd been a recent storm. The beach was littered with flotsam and jetsam and looked like a rubbish tip. There were plastic buckets and bottles, buoys and bits of junk as far as we could see. Our landing could be more aptly described as bouncing and buffeting to a heaven-sent stop.

We positioned ourselves close in to the dunes, set up our little tent, and anchored down the wing of the trike because we could see a storm brewing on the horizon. That night all hell broke loose, and I thought we were going to be swept away in the hammering rain and constant lightning strikes. Our little igloo was being battered relentlessly and let in the water. Needless to say, we had no sleep.

Calm came with the dawn, and when we surfaced we saw an older couple making their way to us along the beach. They had seen us land the previous evening and had come to invite us to breakfast at their home. They drove us to their lovely house overlooking the beach, where they had prepared a beautifully laid dining table with a scrumptious smorgasbord breakfast. It was a magic morning and flight home—after refuelling—and was worth every bit of tousle and tumble along the way. It was one of many bold, fun adventures that I shared with Joe.

Daniel Pink, author of *The Power of Regret*, talks about the top five regrets people have, and not being bold is one of them. In a survey of thousands of people, most regretted inaction more than action over the long term: not being bold enough in the work place or relationships, not following through with an idea, not making new friends, not taking on a challenge. Over the long term, people regret what they don't do rather than what they do.

Boldly walking through life is a powerful force. Boldness inspires me. When I encounter someone who is comfortable in their skin, who boldly states their opinions and speaks from their authenticity, I feel relaxed. I feel safe. At times I am in absolute awe of them. Passionate people, who honestly and enthusiastically tell you what they think and what turns them on, are infectious and invigorating to me. Whenever I move boldly forward I feel strong, discerning and protected. When I trust my gut, opportunities and miracles show up.

How cruel it is that after an unhappy childhood, many people continue to beat themselves up, play small, stay fearful, ignore their desires, or behave in ways that translate to *I don't matter*. A life-changing alternative to carrying an unhealed lesion around throughout life is to boldly walk forward while proudly baring your scars. Kahlil Gibran wrote: 'Out of suffering have emerged the strongest souls; the most massive characters are seared with scars.'

Being bold builds confidence.

To speak my truth and live boldly has been a monumental evolution for me, from the sad, suppressed and lonely child that I was, to the coping and disordered personality that I was, to the self-rejecting adult I grew into, to the newly faceted human I am today who understands my unhappy adoption/separation story and is rewriting it.

Let's be bold and act according to our values, share our feelings, stand up and speak out on matters that matter to us, trust our instincts and honour our selves.

The world needs bold people to pave the way to a more conscious compassionate society.

19

Know Your Vulnerabilities and Triggers

'The reason you can't move forward is that you keep applying an old formula to a new level in your life. Change the formula to get a different result.'

—Emily Maroutian

Adoptees had to develop coping strategies to deal with what happened to us. It was necessary for us to manage the trauma of separation and work out ways to adapt to our adoptive families. However, in our adult lives, applying previously useful, outdated coping strategies to current triggering situations can seriously hinder us in the present. Learning about our vulnerabilities and triggers is an important step in re-evaluating our thoughts and behaviours that may actually be part of our coping modus operandi.

Ask yourself what really rattles you. When you look back over your life and relationships, can you see repetitive patterns that show up, periodically playing out with spooky regularity?

It might seem as though the universe is conspiring against you, and that no matter how hard you try to be nice, to please, to avoid, to change, the same scenario shows up again and again. A big fat black cloud appears out of the blue. You were happy, your life was on track—or you were feeling okay, at least—and bang, someone or something throws you sideways.

It might seem like an insignificant trigger to anyone else. It could be something as simple as a slip of the tongue by someone in your circle, or an absence of reassuring words when you need some bolstering. It could be that you feel betrayed, ignored or unloved by someone.

Reflecting on the details of activating events helps us to see whether we are echoing outmoded protective, defensive behaviours. Otherwise we will keep repeating the same scenarios until the lesson has been learned and we move on.

One of my core sensitivities is safety. I feel safe with people who meet me with openness and warmth. When I sense that other people are relaxed and real, I feel safe. But if I'm met with any kind of rejection, invalidation, hostility or just an impersonal guard, I feel it acutely. I could be knocked off centre by even a hint of rejection. It would feel like a blow to the belly, or like my heart had hit the floor. Followed by some degree of anxiety, my impulse was always to retreat or fight. Many people who have suffered the trauma of abandonment in childhood will understand this vulnerability.

But it's unrealistic to shield ourselves from places and people who make us feel unsafe; I know, I've tried. After all, we can't stay home 24/7. We're always going to come up against unfriendly, nasty, cold, angry and uncaring people, people who rub salt into our particular wounds. At these times of derailment, it's helpful to have a strategy. It's also helpful to remember the words and wisdom of Don Miguel Ruiz, who wrote the timeless and truthful book, *The Four Agreements*.

One of the four agreements is: 'Don't take anything personally.' Everyone is running and projecting their own story out into the world and into relationships. Their perceptions are filtered through their subjective narrative. What others think of us, how they treat us, what they believe about us, is their choice. Taking responsibility for the unkind or insensitive words of someone else perpetuates the belief that we are at fault for the feelings of others, and we dismiss ourselves in the process.

Some time ago I felt gutted when someone lied to me and spoke in a hostile manner. My safety and security were threatened when they tried to undermine my stay at a writer's retreat I had just settled into. I was caught off-guard when this person made it clear that he didn't want me there, even though my space was very separate from his, and I had a firm arrangement with the owner of the retreat. After feeling safe and happy the day before this happened, I was suddenly dumped into the deep end of my trauma memory. Not feeling welcome, safe and secure made me feel very distressed. I felt so uncomfortable that I didn't sleep well that night, wondering if and why the guy didn't like me, and thinking that I'd leave in the morning, retreat ruined.

The next day, after my nervous system had calmed down and I'd had time to reassess, I gathered myself and intercepted the old fight-or-flight pattern with the thought: *I'm staying put*. This man was not going mess up my plan. I had a pre-arrangement, a valid reason to be there, so he could go jump. It was important to detach from my reactivity and take affirmative action to stand my ground and assert my boundary. I had to claim my space.

In the past I would have either turned tail and left, or argued and defended, which would probably have made the situation worse. Pausing rather than reacting was my best strategy—taking time out for emotions to subside so that frontal-lobe thinking could re engage.

Claiming our space and strengthening our boundaries is important for adoptees, who may have felt neither here nor there for so long and might not feel fleshed out enough to hold ground. When we determinedly contradict an old narrative that scripts us as less than, we can build boundaries and personal power.

We are, either consciously or unconsciously, directing the movie of our life, and drawing actors and extras to play various parts. When people come into our orbit and press our buttons, this usually signifies that we are recreating familiar scenes from the past, giving us yet another opportunity to put things right.

This is called repetition compulsion: being unconsciously drawn again and again to reconstruct the circumstances in which the original trauma occurred. This drive is caused by an urge to rewrite the story of the past and create an empowering resolution to the trauma this time around. Some people will literally reconstruct their former horror on the very date and time of the original traumatic incident. Abuse victims are often drawn to people and circumstances that recreate their trauma in a futile attempt to be loved by the perpetrator.

I have a personal example of this. Some years ago my then boyfriend and I were on a road trip for my birthday. He was one in a line of narcissistic men in my life, beginning with my adoptive father, although my pattern of attracting men who loved themselves too much (a good title for a book) was close to its final fatal phase, thank goodness. Anyway, my boyfriend was smart, charming, handsome, romantic and funny. He was also self-absorbed, dismissive and controlling, and had a silver tongue that made many promises with no actual delivery. In other words, a classic gaslighting, grandstanding, grandiose guy.

We were in a town several hours away from home, and had been invited to spend a night with an acquaintance of his, a man I didn't know and instantly didn't like. This man was a very unnerving character and his house had a darkness to it, energetically and physically. That night was a nightmare for me. There were screaming, scarily aggressive neighbours right outside the window, which made me extremely anxious, and when I expressed my unease I was dismissed by both my boyfriend and his mate, who told me it was just the usual dramas next door, and that I didn't need to worry. They carried on drinking.

My anxiety reached panic level and I was frozen with fear all night. I didn't sleep a wink. Consequently, I was exhausted and cranky the next morning. My boyfriend showed zero empathy, as is usual with a narcissist. So, on my actual birthday we clashed. He got in his car, drove away and left me standing in the street. When I called his phone to make peace, his phone was turned off. He was giving me the familiar silent treatment.

I hung around in the spot where he left me, thinking he would come back and get me. In my mind there was no way he would drive away and actually leave me there. But time went by, and after many calls and messages to his phone, I realised he really had gone.

I collapsed onto a bench seat and my heart fell to the floor. I was devastated. I sat there and reflected on the profundity of my abandonment on my birthday. My old script was playing, once again, yet another version of the story of my birth. None of my desperate calls to get my boyfriend—or my birth mother—to come back had made any impact.

It's eerie how past and present can overlap in this dream we call life. We repeat what we don't repair, setting up re-enactments of the original wounding event in an unwitting effort to resolve the experience. In every replaying of my original trauma, I was cast as unimportant, unworthy and abandoned.

Living in the fog of adoption was living out a recurring dream of despair, loss and grief. It's liberating to wake up, walk out of the fog and break the spell of adoption narrative. By responding differently to triggers, by not reacting the same way we always have, we can change the dynamic and miraculously replace the old replayed story with a new story that we have purposely written and directed in accordance with our authentic aspirations.

I appreciate Joseph Campbell's insights into the universal theme of the hero's journey. As you'll recall from an earlier chapter, this involves three stages: departure, initiation and return. As the protagonist in our story, we are called on a quest. Throughout our life journey we face challenges and struggles that, when overcome, transform us. We then return from our journey with the knowledge gained from lessons learned that we can then share with our families and community.

My adoptee story has taken me through many parts of the world, on rocky roads and equally rocky relationships, experiences that have steadily revealed to me what happened to me when I was born and cast away. This full-circle journey has brought me back to the place where I began, but this time I am whole. I have returned from my odyssey with *me*.

When we understand our own stories better, and the vulnerabilities contained in them, we're able to steadily rewrite an improved narrative. Knowledge is power. The next time a re-stimulating incident occurs, we're ready to slay the dragon. Any perceived foe can be disarmed with a sword of truth.

As Maya Angelou said, 'When we know better we do better.'

20

Forgiven Not Forgotten

> 'Hatred and non-forgiveness is the punishment we give to ourselves. Non-forgiving not only harms us, it gradually destroys us.'
>
> —*The Dance Between Joy and Pain*,
> M Patel and R Goswami

It took me a long time to figure out forgiveness. It seemed like an abstract, namby-pamby, kiss-and-make-up puke fest. A turn-the-other-cheek wimp-out. I saw forgiveness as an unearned gift to the bastards. There was no way the fighter in me was going to forgive. Instead of bestowing forgiveness, I sought revenge, acted out defiantly, raged, or suppressed my fury with alcohol and drugs, and wallowed in a mire of emotional sludge that just served to keep me stuck.

But now I know that forgiveness means something different from my earlier take. It means that I no longer carry anger, blame, resentment or vengeance regarding the sad, bad things that happened in my past, or towards whoever perpetrated the injustices. Which is very healthy—for me. (Forgiveness is good for the forgiver, but not necessarily for the forgiven; they have their own work to do.)

However, forgiveness doesn't mean that we need to condone or forget. It's important to hold people to account, and to remember the past for the lessons learned and to forewarn and forearm us for the future. We can still stand up and fight for what is right and call out the wrongs that are being committed. We can leave a person or a situation that isn't supporting our best. We can advocate for the exploited and abused. And we can still expect redress for the pain and losses that were inflicted on us.

I realised that I could still be a warrior and forgive.

Forgiving *myself* was the most challenging. I recall a miraculous healing session where I forgave myself for circumstances that were not my fault but for which I had taken responsibility. I was abducted and raped when I was fourteen, and I had made it my fault for being out on the street so late at night.

We adoptees can be very hard on ourselves. Guilt can be a constant companion, and shame a skeleton in our closet (I have a black belt in self beat-up). In Voice-Dialogue sessions that I've facilitated, I've spoken to heavyweight inner critics of people who were victimised as children. They endure daily crushing criticism for not being good enough, for not knowing better, or for forgetting to do this or that.

Children tend to take on blame for hurtful experiences and the bad things that happen in their world, and if their feelings are not heard and assuaged by their caretakers they can carry that guilt throughout their lives.

When I think about my first role in life as a Band-Aid baby for my adoptive mother, I see how the not-good-enough, always-striving-to-be-better me was born. The bar was unreachable, because nothing I did would ever make me as good as my mother's imagined natural daughter. But I forgive my dear mother absolutely, because I know she struggled and suffered and tried her best. Even my abusive, narcissistic adoptive father has my forgiveness; his frailty at the end of his life helped because I could see his vulnerability for the first time.

Everyone deserves our love and forgiveness in their vulnerability. We all begin life utterly vulnerable, and that's when we need the best protection and care. Forgiveness is letting go of emotion still attached to painful memories and accepting that shit happens. But it's important to remember that though shit happens, *we* are not shit. Whatever happened to us in childhood was not our fault, and doesn't define who we are.

When the burden of angry baggage, including self-anger, is lifted we have so much more energy available to spend on creating more of what we want in our lives. A life that includes more peace, prosperity and joy.

How can we be a brighter light, rather than a bitter and twisted perpetual victim? How can we be of service to others who may struggle and suffer? How can we rise and shine despite the wrong things we've done and that people have done to us?

By taking the lessons forward: forgiven but not forgotten.

21

Home to the Heart

'The loss of a parent by forceful separation causes extreme psychological harm. Separated from a parent, the child feels fear, abandonment, loss … the end of his or her world, tiny and limited as it is, held together only by a mother's touch and love. Comfort in a hug, security in a loving gaze has disappeared.'

—Phil Kronk

Infants deprived of a mother's loving comfort and bonded connection can have ongoing difficulties in forming and maintaining loving relationships. If, as is the case with many adoptees, they download a deep-seated belief that they are flawed and unworthy of love, they may not recognise love when it comes their way, or be able to let it in.

I knew very little about love for a very long time. Repetition compulsion drove me to choose men who resembled my adoptive father, men who were emotionally immature and unavailable, controlling and narcissistic, and incapable of giving steady, secure love and care. Men like this were familiar to me. I didn't know what a respectful, reciprocal and loving relationship was.

My first relationship was appalling. I had no self-esteem and I believed that man when he told me there was something wrong with me. I took the blame for everything that wasn't working in our relationship. My self-negating monkey mind would take me to the moon and beyond in a matter of moments. A raging, swirling set of self-doubting, suspicious, untrusting, angry, scary, sad, catastrophic thoughts would take my anxiety level from zero to a hundred in seconds. What if, if only, what's the point—fatally flawed loser-type thoughts used to take me on a downward spiral of depression lasting for days. I used alcohol and other substances to counter the pain of those thoughts.

I've since learned that thoughts are only thoughts and I have the power to change them—although sometimes I do need some help. I once told a friend that I felt like a failure because I had reached the all-time low of living in a tent. With infectious positivity and a big smile, she said, 'No, you're not a failure, you're an adventurer.' Immediately I felt better.

Sometimes we need an intercept to turn our habitual thinking around. People who have suffered trauma, abuse or neglect, or who were unloved as children, will have a default pattern of self-doubt, self-neglect, self-berating and unloving self-talk. Coming home to the heart is where all those crazy lies disappear.

The primary work of people who were traumatised in childhood is to come back to and stay grounded in our body, and in our internal centre of self-love. We must deliberately and intentionally work to heal the wounds of our childhood, or we will carry them into our future and limit our experience of love in this life.

Coming home to the heart means prioritising our health, our emotional and spiritual wellbeing, and our needs and desires. It involves creating a balance between giving to our loved ones and giving to ourselves, and noticing distractions that take us away from what we need to focus on, for ourselves.

For me, bringing my attention back to my personal needs and goals takes vigilance and commitment. I've caught myself many times finding every possible distraction known to man when there's something important I need to focus on, something that's for me and my sense of fulfilment and happiness. For instance, I might suddenly think it's imperative to join an online dating site to find a new man. After an hour of scrolling through profiles, I'm invariably so disheartened and despondent that I've lost the will to live! Looking at real estate and finding my dream home can waste another hour. Maybe my dog needs another walk, or I should stock up on kitchen supplies. I can while away hours like this.

My therapist has been great at bringing me back to what's important. She has helped me to find my way back to my body, and to the heart of what really matters to *me*. When I'm back on track, I can see what I need to focus on right at that moment, and my next step to achieving what I want in my life. She helps me to remember what it is that really turns me on and takes me forward.

There's a helpful technique that I found in the book *Happy for No Reason*, by Marci Shimoff, which is to focus on breathing in and out of your heart centre. Breathe in deeply and gently while imagining or saying the words *love, ease, compassion*. I was surprised at how quickly I felt the soothing effect of this simple exercise.

When I'm again drifting away like the untethered astronaut, I find my way back to the home of my heart because, in the words of Rumi, 'Only from the heart can you touch the sky.'

22

Changing the Script

> 'The purpose of Compassionate Enquiry is to drill
> down to the core stories people tell themselves—to
> get them to see what story they are telling themselves
> unconsciously; what those beliefs are, where they came
> from; and guide them to the possibility of letting go of
> those stories, or letting go of the hold those stories have
> on them ... That's what Compassionate Enquiry is.'
>
> —Gabor Maté

I used to be an acquiescent adoptee who had no voice, who didn't rock the boat, and whose primary occupation was to please, appease and impress. I felt like I was an actor in other people's plays, playing scripted roles of their desire. I was a chameleon who could blend into any situation and appear relaxed and confident, but below the surface of my coping persona was a tumult of trepidation and a quagmire of melancholy.

With no sense of self or personal boundary, I was easy game for power players, manipulators, abusers and predators. I had been subjugated and substituted by the adoption system, and mistreated by a cruel and narcissistic adoptive father. I had been trained from birth to be invisible, inaudible and inconsequential.

I acknowledge the validity of my old story: the undermining damage caused by original separation, the physical and emotional abuse by my adoptive father, being abducted and raped at the age of fourteen. My first relationship was another abusive episode. I felt worthless. I didn't deserve to be treated so appallingly. I was a vulnerable victim of exploitation and violence. I had no self-esteem and therefore attracted more hurtful experiences. And, regrettably, I inadvertently hurt others because of my own wounding. Hurt people hurt people.

Throughout my life, I have repeated the sad story of my past in my own mind, and very occasionally to others, mainly therapists, thereby reinforcing its key element: that I was a victim, unimportant and unworthy. My identification with that narrative meant that unconsciously I drew actors into my life who cooperated with my I-don't-deserve script. While not denying the unhappy veracities of my childhood, I now realise that it's important for me not to linger there.

It's important to listen to our own words. What stories are we telling and retelling to ourselves and others? What are we saying about ourselves and our past to others? Taking an objective look at the events of our life, and the messages we've taken on board, allows us to detach from a default narrative.

One day as I was driving I had a revelation. What if I turned around my sorrowful story of suffering and focused on the positive recollections of my past? In my mind I started flipping the old script. I reframed the things I said to myself.

My adoptive parents provided me with a secure home, and an education. I loved having adventures at the beach house that my adoptive father built, where I had the freedom to make cubbies, and have fires on the beach with my brothers and the kids next door.

My mother always lovingly prepared delicious food for us, and I fondly remember her routine Sunday baking when I would stand on a chair and help her stir sweet mixtures, and I was allowed to lick the spoon. Her pies and slices were blue ribbon worthy.

I've travelled. I've been fortunate to live in the most beautiful places, and here I am in awesome Australia.

I am resilient and determined to overcome adversity. I'm proud of my will to do and be better, and of my ability to care for and empathise with others. And ... I'm alive!

I felt so uplifted after thinking this way. Just shifting my perspective had an immediate positive effect on my mood and energy.

I'm not suggesting that we dismiss the realities and hardships of our life; they were real experiences and worthy of respect, but it's important that we not dwell on them. It's important to acknowledge the truth of the unfortunate experiences in our life, but focus on and feed the feel-good aspects.

In a Cherokee legend, an elder tells his grandson about the two wolves battling within all of us. One wolf is evil and represents envy, regret and greed. The other wolf is humble, kind and benevolent. When the boy asks which wolf wins the battle, his grandfather says, 'The one you feed.'

I've read that the brain has a negative bias, which makes us tend to cling to adverse events and memories. Some say that this has evolutionary roots, from a time when it was more important to focus on the (negative) predator in the bush rather than the (positive) pretty flowers growing there. Fear and emotional intensity sharpen our attention, which causes us to remember the details of shocking events more clearly.

I remember the terror of my adoptive father storming toward me, and the shock and pain of being hit repeatedly across my face more than the vague memories of having fun times with my friends.

Scientific research shows that we can train our brains away from negative bias by practising gratitude and staying with the recollection of a happy event for at least twenty or thirty seconds. Spending time absorbing the affirmative in this way disempowers negative bias and reinforces positive patterns in the brain. As George Lucas said, 'Always remember, your focus determines your reality.'

Meeting my father

As you know, when I met my birth mother, it didn't go well. During our meeting she lied to me about who my father was, and I went on a wild goose chase trying to find the man she had whipped up a story about. When my search came up with nothing, I just let it go.

Some time later I wrote to her telling her that I couldn't find anything about the man she'd named, and she replied that she had told me that story because she wished that he *had* been my father. She still wouldn't disclose the real name of my father.

Years later I wrote to her again, this time I spoke with an indignant tone, and this time she finally gave me the truth, but begged me not to contact him, just as she had begged me not to contact her three other daughters.

Even with this information, another few years went by. It's easy to put off something that requires risk, hutzpah, and possible pain.

One day, out of the blue, I was prompted to look up the name she had given me. I wasn't even sure if I could trust that she had told me the truth. Anyway, it didn't take long to discover that this man, whom I'll refer to as M, was the proprietor of an outback pub near the Flinders Ranges in South Australia. It was a long way from Byron Bay. Again, I put the information aside and got on with my life.

Then I met someone at a party who happened to be travelling to South Australia and offered to drive me north from Adelaide to meet M. After the build-up to the anticlimax of meeting D, I decided that I would just go and see this man, and that I would instinctively know in my biological bones whether he really was my father. I had no particular plan; I thought I'd just play it by ear.

So I flew to Adelaide and was picked up from the airport by my friend. Off we drove into the wild blue yonder. It was a three-hour journey north through flat dry country dotted with stone ruins, scraggly trees and vast wheat fields. When we arrived, in front of us was a beautiful, classic old Australian pub. Built in the 1800s, with leadlight windows, bullnose verandas and cast-iron lacework, it stood with stately presence on the corner of the one-street town.

I suddenly started to feel nervous as I grasped how momentous my next steps would be. What had I done? What if this? What if that? What if the other thing? Blah blah blah went my brain.

When I walked through the saloon doors of the pub like a scene from a wild-west movie, right there I met eyes with a gnarly-looking, grey-haired, grey-goateed man standing behind the front bar. There was an impish sparkle in those piercing blue eyes and I knew, there and then, in that moment, that he was my father. I felt it.

His eyes moved back to the patrons in front of him sitting at the bar and he carried on talking. They seemed like locals, and my friend and I were conspicuous blow-ins. We went to another part of the big L-shaped bar and I waited nervously for us to be served. We ordered two beers. I was in my mid-fifties and I was setting eyes on my father for the first time. It all felt surreal.

My anxiety about what I was going to do, how I was going to approach him, and what I was going to say reached a crescendo of crazy stress that literally lifted me off the stool and walked me outside. I paced up and down the pavement for I don't know how long. Then I walked back in and sat down beside my friend, who said, 'Go on, make your move,' or something to that effect.

At that point I looked at the beautiful old wooden jukebox beaming with turquoise lights in the corner of the front bar, and I walked over and chose a couple of songs. Then, to my own amazement, I started dancing around on my own like some look-at-me, over-confident city slicker. The truth was, I was tangled up in turmoil and my body was trying to let off steam.

M looked at me with a wry smile and a glint in his eye. He opened the till and put coins on the bar. 'Play some Dire Straits,' he said.

So I put on 'Sultans of Swing' and swung around to face the bar, at which point I mouthed and motioned to M to meet me at the other end of the bar. He walked to the far end of the bar without hesitation.

I sat on the stool and there we were, face to face, and I hadn't rehearsed anything. He was looking straight into my eyes from a couple of feet away. And this is what came out of my mouth: 'Hi, my name is Rabekah and I was adopted in 1961 and my birth mother, D, from Hamilton in Victoria, tells me that you are my father.'

Kapow.

M took a moment and then hung his head for a couple of seconds. When he looked up he said, 'I'm sorry that I don't recall her. I used to travel with my footy team and I was a bit of a root rat.'

M's lumpy arthritic hands, with an equally lumpy gold nugget on his ring finger, rested on the bar while he told me a little about his life, which included a tragedy that still haunted him with sad regret decades later. He said that he had health problems, and that one day in the not-to-distant future he will have 'gone fishing' and won't be coming back. He paused for a moment, and then said, 'If I am your father, then what do we do?' Straightaway he answered his own question. 'Well, we can be friends.'

No words can express the deep sigh I felt in that moment. My whole body and soul relaxed and rejoiced in his acceptance of me.

When I went upstairs to the room that M had given us, I was so elated that I jumped up and down on the old spring bed like a kid, bouncing and bursting with joy. M was my kinda guy. My dad, a loveable larrikin. I was sooo happy.

The next morning I met his beautiful, hulking mastiff-type dog. I love dogs; he loved dogs. Another match! I was so excited. What a dream.

We said goodbye with the plan to organise a DNA test. I sailed away on cloud nine and when I got back home to the Byron Shire I sent M an email. It was a pleasant exchange, and he confirmed that he would enquire about a paternity test.

I was so relieved to have found a cooperative openhearted man after such a hard and heartless meeting with D. My father would be my friend and I could learn all about my French ancestry. We would hang out, talk and get to know each other. Maybe I could help him out in the pub. Whatever. It proved to me that good shit *can* happen to counteract the bad shit.

In 2014 I received an email from M. It was a short message telling me that he didn't want to complicate in any way the rest of his life, and on that basis he must say no to any more involvement.

Signed off with, *See ya*, M.

I don't remember how long I sat in front of my computer with my heart on the floor.

There really are no words to describe how I felt.

Crestfallen falls short.

What I feel now, with some distance from that time, is a deep disappointment and a healthy smattering of righteous anger. And it's not particularly personal anger. M was a good bloke. I really liked him. He was honest and earthy and wore his heart on his sleeve, and that's the kind of man I respect.

My anger is more broadly related to the injustice that adoptees have been and still are subjected to. We are still being dismissed, disrespected and treated so insensitively, even by the people who created us. Where is their accountability? After all, they had sex and created a baby, there needs to be some ownership of that fact. Where is the empathy and regard? How many adoptees like me have been so careful, so considerate and respectful of our biological and adoptive parents' feelings?

I've had enough of pussyfooting around people who don't take responsibility for their actions, and who don't care about the feelings of their offspring. When was it taken for granted that adoptees should be acquiescent and accepting and not rock anyone's boat? I suggest we do start rocking those boats; they're already way off kilter. A bit of righteous anger can go a long way to changing the endemic inequities in the lives of adoptees.

11 ingredients

Despite the inevitable vicissitudes of life, I believe that life is a feast to enjoy. This is my tried and true recipe for a richer banquet made up of these eleven ingredients:

1. Truth

> 'Truth is like the sun. You can shut it out
> for a time but it ain't going away.'
>
> —Elvis Presley

The highs and lows, the fears, pains, joys and loves, losses and grief. Ask yourself if the messages you were told when you were growing up are true. How were you influenced to feel about yourself? Were you made to feel unimportant or valued? What were the underlying feelings you carried as a child? Have you carried messages about yourself from childhood into adulthood?

In an interview, actress Jane Fonda had this to say: 'It doesn't matter what the objective reality is, it's how you were made to feel about yourself in childhood.' John Bradshaw says, 'You can't heal what you can't feel.' Acknowledging the realities of our childhood experiences is the first step out of the fog towards finding our authentic self. Alex Haley said, 'Either you deal with what is the reality, or you can be sure that the reality is going to deal with you.' We can save ourselves a lot of repetitious re-wounding experiences once we get clear about our past.

As an adoptee, you may have been gaslit for so long that the truth might have to be dug out from under the layers of internalised untruths. Understanding the truth of our past wounding experiences allows us to put our feelings into context, and our past will no longer be an unconscious obsession and influence in our present.

In the words of Brendan Burchard, 'Someone who lives a "charged life" is informed about but not confined by the past.' The truth sets us free to be ourself and to experience more light and love in our life.

Truth telling empowers. Truth forms the solid foundation upon which we can build a more expanded life that reflects our genuine values and desires.

2. Support

> 'Your support network is the solid ground from which you can propel yourself upwards.'
>
> —Anna Barnes

A support network can include counsellors, friends, support groups, adoption therapists, teachers and mentors. Surrounding ourselves with people who uplift us, who have our back, who believe in and inspire us are the people to bring in and keep close.

I look back with sadness at some extremely tough times in my life when I was all on my own. A new friend helped me to realise that support exists, and all I had to do was research and reach out. It has made a huge difference in my life to be able to receive help.

Therapy has been a wonderful support in my life. In an interview, the actress Sandra Bullock said, 'Therapy is like washing your brain. If you're willing to get a facial then wash your brain. Clean it and get rid of anything that no longer belongs there.' I carried so many conflicting thoughts in my adoptee brain, and therapy has taught me how to detach from them and come back to my centre.

You don't have to feel alone. There's help: on the phone, in the community, in nature. Nature is a wonderful soothing balm for the soul. There are so many books and YouTube videos offering support, wisdom and love. In particular, I love Gabor Maté's gentle wisdom.

3. Expression

>'Express yourself, don't repress yourself.'
>
>—MADONNA

Give voice to your untold stories. Truth telling empowers us and it informs society and the next generations. Feel and release emotions. All our feelings are worthy of expression. Repressing ourselves can keep us small and invisible, to ourselves and to others. Repression definitely dampens our energy and enthusiasm for life.

Expression defines who we are. Finding safe and creative ways to emote and express is invigorating. Writing, painting, drawing, cooking, drumming, gardening, singing ... the list is endless. Having a passion project of some kind, anything that allows us to connect to and reveal our creative self will infuse us with energy.

Feeling *all* of our feelings is healthy. This includes unpleasant feelings like regret and sadness. Accepting the suffering in our life is just as important as appreciating the happy times. Having a positive, optimistic attitude doesn't have to exclude the more unsavoury realities of life. Healthy expression is acknowledging the full range of emotions.

Anger can be a powerful expression for change—if it's clean, present anger.

If it's old rage-full kind of anger it needs to be expressed safely and preferably with professional support.

Oh, and practising the power of *fuck off* is invaluable. I say it every day—to the mosquito, to the computer, to the latest shit show on the news, in my head to the rude person in front of me ... There are endless opportunities to improve this phenomenal form of expression. Billy Connolly is a great inspiration.

4. Compassionate forgiveness

> 'We all make mistakes, don't we? But if you can't forgive yourself, you will always be an exile in your own life.'
>
> —Curtis Sittenfeld

When I learned to forgive myself, it felt like a huge, heavy burden was lifted off me. Being compassionate and forgiving of ourselves is most important for adoptees, who may have taken on guilt and shame related to their abandonment, or for wanting to search for their biological families, or for not feeling 'special' and 'lucky'. We need to be kind to and accepting of ourselves and stop making ourselves wrong or bad.

It's important to forgive, to learn, and to let go of past adversities and mistakes. Reflect honestly on the situation and see how we might have done better. Is it even our fault? Are we truly accountable? It's okay to feel regret. Regret is not a dirty word, unlike shame, which makes us feel unworthy, bad or wrong. Regret involves a responsible sense of viewing and assessing the situation and seeing that there could have been a more desirable outcome. Regrets can be important lessons to take forward in life. As the Irish say, 'Hindsight is the best insight to foresight.'

My regrets used to cause me to beat myself up mercilessly until I realised how unnecessary repeated self-punishment was. Forgiveness, on the other hand, lets us learn and grow. When we know better, we can do better.

I've forgiven the ignorant and abusive forced-adoption scheme that colluded to remove babies from their mothers. What's done is done, and the best way to channel my feelings regarding the injustices of forced adoption is to use my voice for change. We can all learn from that huge mistake and help to pave a better way forward.

Adoption has been my life lesson, and although I will keep learning I've let go of the pain, loss, and cognitive dissonance that used to keep me stuck. Staying angry, hurt and helpless doesn't make amends. All it does is make us suffer, over and over again.

Forgiveness involves changing any harsh inner dialogue that's imbued with blame, shame, criticism and anger. Know that you are trying to do and be your best, and that even though you have made mistakes in the past and will make more in the future, you are a normal, worthy and loveable human. Forgive yourself and move on with self-encouragement. Be kind, gentle and loving with yourself at all times. Talk to yourself as you would to a child. Forgive.

5. Boundaries

> 'When you say "yes" to others, make sure you are not saying "no" to yourself.'
>
> —Paulo Coelho

Personal boundaries include knowing what you want, and what you will and won't accept in your world, being clear about what and who you will open your door to or say yes to, and learning where and when you need to say no. Boundaries include acting on your gut feelings, i.e. intuition, drawing your line in the sand, and letting events and people go if they bring you down.

Boundaries can be set and expressed in love. Speak from love, always. When you care for and respect yourself, you will speak lovingly on your own behalf. You could say, for example, 'If you continue to talk to me in that way I'll have to leave.' Or, 'I appreciate your opinion but I'm not willing to change my mind. Clearly expressing our boundaries builds respect, value and safety.

Boundaries include resting when we feel tired rather than pushing on regardless. Making our wellbeing a priority makes it easier for us to know what to say yes or no to, or to negotiate a win-win outcome. As someone who once had no idea what a personal boundary was, and who was open to manipulation and exploitation, I can now attest to the power of boundaries to increase self-protection and wellbeing.

I like what Anita Moorgani says about boundaries. She says that if you lack self-love and care, you will have diminished chi (life-force energy) and be more susceptible to illness and less protected from ill-intended people. By expanding your chi, you will naturally have better boundaries. Increasing your self-love will have the flow-on effect of creating a stronger energy field, which will organically filter out unhealthy depleting energies and allow in higher forces.

6. Taking charge/self-empowerment

> 'Self-empowerment is seeking a solution
> rather than fixating on the problem.'
>
> —Bobbi Morgan

Decades ago someone said to me, 'No one can do it for you.' Although I've forgotten the context (I was probably complaining about something), I have always remembered this simple statement. It encapsulates the lesson I've learned over and over throughout my life: my health and happiness are entirely up to me. Complaining, shaming and blaming bolsters victimhood; I know it's easy to go there.

Noticing when our thoughts increase our victim status is a crucial step toward reclaiming our personal power. We may have been a victim in the past, but we can now choose self-empowerment. Through our commitment to self-care and forgiveness, and by adopting an optimistic attitude, we will take back our power.

Simply taking dedicated action toward our goals, no matter how big or small they are, can be empowering. Meeting challenges head on and working our way through them, finding ways to help ourselves achieve our desires, or even fixing the washing machine when it stops working (one of my proudest moments). Every time we finish what we set out to do, every time we give something our all, even if we don't succeed, and every time we get back up after a fall we are building personal power.

Baba Jolie says that what you think about, you bring about. If you disempower and undermine yourself with thoughts of not being good enough, or not having what it takes to achieve something you want, that's what you will reaffirm as your reality. Letting go of disempowering inner dialogue, beliefs and behaviours is transformative. Follow what empowers you. Acknowledge your fears, but don't let them stop you from moving onward and upward, in the words of Buzz Lightyear (arm outstretched, reaching for the stars), 'to infinity and beyond!'

7. Positive self-talk

> 'Whatever words we utter should be chosen with care.'
>
> —BUDDHA

What words are you uttering to yourself daily? Out of an average sixty thousand thoughts a day, the majority will be repetitive and negative—on average, eighty percent. One positive practice is to write down some usual negative thoughts and then replace each one with a positive. Changing our internal dialogue to the affirmative is a fundamental part of changing our life.

Notice the critical voices in your head that say things like *You're too sensitive* or *Get over it* or *You're not good enough* or *You're stupid*. Maybe they're more subtle messages, like *You always* ... or *You never* ... Self-judgment and criticism will erode self-confidence, mental health and life force. It's up to us to create and inhabit a bubble of positivity or negativity. Telling ourselves that we are forever flawed will keep us stuck in a stagnant cesspit of self-pity.

When we choose to no longer be defined by our hurtful experiences, past mistakes, problems or imperfections, our inner light will begin to take on a new shine. By creating a climate of compassion through our loving self-talk, negativity will become a thing of the dark past as we grow more into the light. And the light is the truth; it conveys the message that we are who we are, with no judgment attached. We were shaped by our experiences, positive and negative. We have strengths and weaknesses, and despite and including all of this, we are human and we are enough.

8. Physical care

> 'Take care of your body, it's the only place you have to live.'
>
> —Jim Rohn

I know I'm stating the obvious here, but it's good to be reminded of things that matter. I think of our physical bodies as mobile pieces of real estate on this planet. With maintenance, improvements, extensions (or not), and interior and exterior decorating, we can increase their value and get the most out of our once-in-a-lifetime investment opportunity. We can enhance or degrade our earthly abode, personally and more broadly.

Listening to our body, paying attention to how our body is feeling, eating foods that nourish us. Exercise; move every day in a way that feels good. Don't exhaust yourself. Tailor your exercise to suit you. Walking, yoga, boxing ... do what suits your individual body needs.

Movement increases motivation. After years of persuasion and resistance to taking antidepressants, I found that running on the beach cured my depression. I recently ran on the beach in the pouring rain and then jumped into the swirling bubbling ocean. I felt so invigorated.

Instead of putting our physical care on the back burner, we need to prioritise our health. Dental care, breathing fresh air, taking long baths, getting massages, taking a jiu-jitsu class ... your body will thank you for the attention. Physical care increases energy, immunity, mental health and quality of life. Rest when you need to. Sleep well.

9. Grounding

'But it turns out that people who are grounded and secure don't change much under stress. That's what being grounded means.'

—Michael Gruber

My understanding of being grounded is when I'm present in my breath and body, and in the here-and-now reality. When we feel stressed, overwhelmed or overloaded, it can be a soothing, stabilising practice to stop and ground ourselves. Grounding means settling into a relaxed and connected sense of our self. Grounding delivers us from fear and from our mad monkey mind. A walk on a beach or elsewhere in nature, exercising and paying full attention to our body as we do, practising yoga, having a massage, or simply focusing on our feet on the ground while taking long deep breaths: grounding enables us to refocus on what's happening in the present moment.

Grounding has been a big challenge in my life. There is nothing more un-grounding than to be taken from the solid ground of your mother. In shamanic terms I was a lost soul, literally. My school reports would say that if I didn't spend so much time looking out of the window daydreaming I might make more progress with my schoolwork. I was rarely if ever present in the here and now. I was here and somewhere else at the same time, straddling two worlds.

From childhood, the best coping strategy I had was to spend time in nature or with my animal friends. These were the only times I remember feeling at peace. I didn't consciously know that I was grounding myself. Feeling like a ghost among properly fleshed-out human beings, it was a great relief to be alone in the silence and tranquillity of nature, or cuddling my dog.

Dogs are awesome. I've always lived with a dog because I feel relaxed with them. Dogs are great therapy. They are solid beings who know who they are, and they are a hundred percent present. And they are endlessly and unconditionally loving and loyal. Hugging a dog is very grounding. One of my greatest joys is to hug my big beautiful chocolate Labrador, Coco. It's no coincidence that *dog* spelled backwards is *god*.

Barefoot running on the beach, drumming, yoga, writing are some of my favourite ways to ground. What are yours? Another great grounding practice for me is to talk to another adoptee. Hearing other adoptees tell their stories is always grounding for me. Speaking with people who really hear and empathise is deeply healing and anchoring.

Eating well is another way to ground. Preparing a meal with all my attention is soothing and settling. Drinking alcohol and taking drugs isn't. One is an into-body experience and the other is an out-of-body trip. I know how fantastic it is to get out of it. I've been there many times. But I've had to stop those habits in their tracks and replace them with ones that bring me clarity and energy.

A far less appealing way to ground is to be suddenly shocked back into our bodies. Accident or illness can be a sure, albeit painful, way to reinhabit the body.

A few years ago I broke my back after slipping and falling down stairs. I came back to earth extremely hard. I had been running on empty after sleepless nights and constant caring for others, and I was exhausted. I had even cancelled scheduled time away on my own because I thought my family needed me. They didn't. I was on automatic pilot, making others my focus instead of myself.

While I lay flat on my back on a hospital bed, unable to move, I reviewed my life. I saw how I had abandoned myself, again, driven by my habitual other-centred agenda. I had been ignoring my body's signals to rest and recuperate in favour of making sure everyone else was being taken care of, but it was me who needed taking care of. It was an extreme example of 'Pay attention or pay the price'.

Nothing changes if nothing changes. Sometimes we have to push against the tide of our old habits. Prioritising our physical wellness and staying grounded are building blocks for a strong foundation. And as Gordon Hinckley once said, *'You can't build a great building on a weak foundation.'*

10. Finding Fun

> 'We are game-playing, fun-having creatures,
> we are the otters of the universe.'
>
> —Richard Bach

It's so important to have fun. Most of us need more of it. Doing things that are playful and bring laughter and lightness is the best medicine. Life's rather dull without fun. Remember what you enjoyed in your past that you may have forgotten, and bring those elements back into your life. One of my favourites is to hang out with good friends, having a yarn and a laugh. What a joy it is to kid around with people you can relax and vibe with. Life's serious enough; it's fun that's often lacking.

Watching stand-up comedy can be a great tonic. Or dancing, dressing up and going out to a swingers' party. Seriously, if kinky sex is your thing I hope you will get out there and have fun. Whatever it is that appeals to you. More fun makes a lighter, brighter you.

New and exciting experiences can really shake and wake us up. Jumping out of a plane isn't my idea of fun, but for some people it is (I've done it and it was dreadful). Board games and card games can be fun, especially playing in teams. As Joe used to say, 'We're not here for a long time, we're here for a good time.'

11. Stay awake to our dreams

> 'What you radiate outward in your thoughts, feelings, mental pictures and words, you attract into your life.'
>
> —Catherine Ponder

If we keep our dreams in our mind's eye, we will automatically move towards them and they will magnetically attract. Create visions and goals for our life and stay true to them. Having a dream of our best life with all the elements that bring us happiness and a sense of fulfilment becomes our guiding light that we move towards. In my experience, whenever I've been clear and determined to achieve a desired outcome, divine support is at my back.

It helps to dream up the feelings associated with our wish. For example, feel the peace washing over you while you lie in bed and listen to the sounds of the ocean on Spotify. And while you're there, visualise living near the beach with a gorgeous man or woman who adores you. Imagine the sense of contentment settling into your mind and body. (Whoops, I'm getting carried away with my own dream.)

This stuff works. As Jen Sincero says, what you choose to focus on becomes your reality. For me, these self-loving, transformative techniques needed to be learned from scratch and practised with persistence, and I've discovered that every effort invested in self-care is rewarded with renewed vigour.

23

Alchemy

'You are an alchemist; make gold of that.'

—WILLIAM SHAKESPEARE

Turning base metal into gold is a good analogy for transforming whatever has happened to us into something of value so that we sparkle and radiate out into the world. No matter what our past misfortunes, we can still make the most of this precious life.

I recently read *Beneath the Waves*, by Layne Beachley, world-champion surfer and adoptee. Among other things, mostly surfing, Layne talks about her anger, frustration and determination, as well as her loss and grief. She had lost two mothers by the age of seven, when her adoptive mother died suddenly after an operation. She talks openly about her abandonment issues and doing therapy later in her life.

Mainly, the book is about her focus on becoming the world's best female surfer. Her drive to become the best was very much about wanting to feel worthy and loved. I love the motivational saying that she posted on her wall: 'From adversity comes greatness.' Her life is an inspiration and an example of turning early adversity into shining success.

I once did a stand-up comedy performance in Byron Bay, and in my introduction I quoted a supposedly Russian saying that I'd heard and loved with dark delight: 'Life's hard, but at least it's short.' I still love it. That was exactly how I used to feel. Life was hard work with little respite, and death would come as a great relief.

I no longer subscribe to the belief that we have to soldier on and suffer through life, or merely exist. Despite the ups and downs, left-field losses, shocking events and crappy relationships, life really is a gift to enjoy. Whether we savour life's opportunities and pleasures or bemoan our perceived lot is our choice.

Ideally, a newborn grows and flourishes out of a fertile ground of connection, calm and safety. The baby becomes a confident child, and then an adult who has a solid sense of self, self-worth and security. This is the ideal. What can we do now to regain what we lost?

The only way we can achieve what we have lost is to give it to ourselves. Jack Canfield, author of the major bestseller *Chicken Soup for the Soul*, says that we need to stop believing outside forces are controlling our lives and bring the power back to ourselves. By clearing out limiting beliefs, and by understanding ourselves and our strengths, sensitivities, talents, needs, and likes and dislikes without judgment, we can re-form. Honouring ourselves, practising discernment, setting boundaries, going for what we want in life will override any faulty narrative that may have held us back in the past. And we need to find supportive people who want the best for us; we deserve to have people around us who lift us up and cheer us on. We can begin by being our own cheerleader.

Nobel laureate Pearl S Buck writes, 'There is an alchemy in sorrow. It can be transmuted into wisdom, which, if it does not bring joy, can yet bring happiness.'

Let joy be our inner guidance system. Embrace practices that bring us peace and expand our chi. It might be a meditation practice, time in nature, a spiritual retreat or stirring music. By bringing in more and more fulfilling, stress-free and heartening experiences we can literally change the neural pathways in our brain and form patterns of positivity.

If we're feeling down, we can choose to turn our mood around by reading an inspiring book, talking to a friend, going for a run, or listening to the bright calls of the birds outside the window.

I have a friend who suffered the sudden loss of his father when he was very young, and a few years later he and his brother were in a terrifying light-plane crash in New Zealand. He surfs for his mental and physical health, and whenever he feels that his post-trauma symptoms are getting the better of him, an ocean swim or surf brings him back to feeling centred and strong.

Changing self-dialogue to gentle, curious and compassionate language is a big part of positive transformation. Our thoughts become our reality. They are self-perpetuating. Negative thoughts will take us down a slippery spiral to a place I know so well: the black abyss of despair, and it's cold, dark and lonely down there.

Positive thoughts will take us on an upward spiral toward the light. I'm not being unrealistic here. I know that unwelcome events can happen in our life, despite our good intentions, best self-care and an optimistic outlook. But when those things happen we will be far better fortified, and have greater resilience to get through them, when we have a strong connection to our internal light.

Maya Angelou said, 'You will face many defeats in life, but don't let yourself be defeated.'

24

Uncomfortable Truths

> 'In the long run, the most unpleasant truth is a far safer companion than a pleasant falsehood.'
>
> —Theodore Roosevelt

Adoption involves the brutal procedure of mother-infant amputation. Severing a baby from their mother at birth is an unnatural and immoral act. Forced adoption is responsible for complex and long-term injuries to adoptees. Forced adoption is a crime that has sentenced innumerable adoptees to a life of fractured connection to their authentic selves.

Adoptees have been deliberately denied the truth of their ancestry and had their identities erased by way of secrecy and replacement birth certificates. Their identities were stolen; they have been lied to, gaslit, condescended to and treated inequitably.

Our society rightly demonises the marketing of children, child abuse and neglect, yet it hasn't acknowledged that millions of adoptees around the world have suffered all of these injustices. Adoptee lives have been lost. Adoptee lives have been burdened by secrecy, and adoptees struggle with belonging and attachment, and mental and interpersonal issues. Adoptee lives have been hampered by trauma and dislocation at birth.

Adoptee separation trauma is real and needs to be recognised and redressed. Adoptee restoration is justly deserved and well overdue. How can adoptees be compensated for such immorality, such a primal injury, such profound loss?

The *other* stolen generation

The term 'stolen generation' refers not only to the severance of infants from their mothers but also to adopted children who have had their origins and identities stolen from them. In Joss Shawyer's book, Death by Adoption, she states: 'The very act of adoption is a denial of the right of the child to her natural heritage—her birthright—the most basic right a person has, to know who she is.'

All trace of the newborn's history and origin were sealed in closed records so the adoptive parents could 'pretend' that the adopted child was a natural extension of themselves. The adoptee had to take on the name of adopted parents with the issuance of a superseded birth certificate. In many adoptive families, the subject of adoption was never spoken about, and the adoptees had to accept the concealment of their true past and cooperate with the act.

The complex ramifications of adoption practices go much deeper than the erasure of the adoptee's name and original birth certificate. Closed adoption left an indelible mark on the psyche of those it victimised. Many adoptees had their sense of self-worth stolen from them, and they continue to bear the effects of devaluation of self.

One of the most painful and lasting legacies of adoption practice for adoptees has been the difficulty in making and maintaining connection. Connection is something that many adoptees have to work hard at achieving and more often than not struggle with feeling disconnected and separate. The embedded fear of abandonment stands in the way of intimacy for many, leading to isolation, loneliness and depression. In The Tangled Triangle, Gordon Hammond writes: 'If you look closely at our behaviour, you will see that most of it revolves around relationships-connection.' When the connection between mother and child is severed at birth, the ensuing and invisible after-effects of that trauma and loss permeate every subsequent relationship.

My children have grown up with no connection to their grandparents, aunts, uncles, cousins and ancestors on my side. Disconnection is repeated through the generations if we don't intercede and preserve the primal powerful mother-infant bond and accompanying family ties.

The prevailing denial in society, and in the health and legal systems, of the need to address the inequalities in the lives of adoptees has left victims of forced-adoption practice out in the cold, with little acknowledgement or assistance for the damage caused to their lives. Adoptees are still a relatively invisible and subdued sector of the community, and are still not afforded the same legal and human rights as non-adopted people. AM Homes, adoptee and author of The Mistress's Daughter, believes that one of the pathological complications of adoption is that 'adoptees don't have rights; their lives are about supporting the secrets, the needs, and desires of others'. It is time to respect and address the needs of birth mothers and adoptees, whose lives have been seriously altered by the forced-adoption system.

Near-death experience

Adopted people experienced birth and death in their first moments. Their mother/sustenance was gone in a shocking instant. Through hearing stories of near-death experiences, I've come to understand what happened to me and why it has taken me so long to fully reinhabit my body and my life.

My postnatal near-death experience was brought to my semi-conscious awareness when I was in hospital in Melbourne, the day before meeting my mother. I was simultaneously a 29-year-old woman in a hospital bed recovering from an anaphylactic episode, and a newborn lying in a crib after being detached from my life support. I was in the dreamy state of being in two places at once. I was in a timeless place where past, present and future were coexisting. I was outside of time. It was a place of peace.

I've had many weird experiences in my life where it's like I enter the 'other side'. My recollection of myself as a newborn is of lying in the cold and disconnected environment of a hospital nursery cot, and feeling bereft and barely attached to this world. I was hovering in between worlds, with no body to hold me and keep me there. The body of my mother that I had been attached to had gone. I had no lifeline. No boundary, protection and/or anchor. I felt myself floating. Drifting lightly away. I can still remember that feeling.

Then I felt myself being lifted by an unseen support that took over and began to breathe me. Something else was breathing me. With that breath, I was being brought back into my body. I was being breathed. I know it wasn't me. It was something else.

Throughout my adult life I've been intrigued by stories of near-death experiences. And what has fascinated me most is when people talk about the message they heard while floating blissfully above their bodies. The message was often that they had to go back, that it wasn't their time and they had more to do. Whenever I've heard accounts of near-death experiences, this part in particular resonates with me. In my own experience, I was peacefully leaving a suffering body, going back home to a sense of warm connection when something intervened and brought me back. It seemed beyond my control. This experience stayed with me as a perceptive awareness of the unseen mystery of life, a spiritual dimension beyond this physical existence.

I like Shirley MacLaine's explanation of 'the mysterious, non-physical realm that we can't thump on but know exists'. My sense of the spiritual realm has been an ever-present saviour in my life. I acknowledge all the times I have asked for help and the divine has answered.

I recall the time when I was hopelessly lost in a forest after veering off track. I had taken myself off to a remote solo retreat to fast in solitude for a few days. I went to the middle of nowhere and set up camp in a thick forest in a national park. All I had was water and apples. Crazy, I know. Those were the days when I felt so alien and anxious that I would seek out the comfort of solitude to try and regain my sanity. It was hard work just coping in life.

On about day three, I was feeling pretty high from not eating much food when I decided to go for a walk. At some point I realised that the path had disappeared, and I was trudging through the bush with no idea where I was or what direction I was going in. Worried, I turned around and walked back to find the path I'd started on, but I just seemed to be getting further off course. I walked on for some time until I felt exhausted and despairing as the light started to fade. I sat down, realising that I was in serious trouble. I knew it would get cold when night fell and I had nothing to keep me warm. I had the scary thought that I could die from exposure and low blood sugar.

I sat down, put my head in my hands and silently pleaded for help. I begged with all of my being. Suddenly I felt a compulsion to stand, and without thinking I began to walk. I had no idea what direction I was headed in. I just walked. Within a few minutes I came upon the path. I'll never forget that miracle. It was as though I had an unseen guide.

Another time I was driving on an unfamiliar country road to visit a friend. I didn't have a GPS back then so I was relying on a map and the directions my friend had given me. After a while I became aware that I'd taken a wrong turn, and as I looked for a good spot to turn around I came across a rolled car. It was on its side and there was an older woman still inside. I called an ambulance and comforted the woman while we waited for help to arrive. I was in the right place at the right time that day.

There have been many mysterious and miraculous moments in my life where there have been divine intervention and synchronicities. Swiss psychiatrist Carl Jung coined the term 'synchronicity' a century ago, believing strongly that we are all intimately connected via a collective universal consciousness.

Despite living with the problems of PATSD, and having felt a tenuous sense of belonging in this world, I have been regularly reminded that I'm spiritually connected to a greater power and that I'm never really alone. I'm grateful for the unseen benevolent forces that have come to my aid so many times in my life. I wouldn't be here without that power.

We are spiritual beings in a human body in a physical world. Knowing this has been my saviour. Having a bigger-picture perspective has not only been a comfort, but has also made my life far more interesting. I've had intuitive insights to direct me, inexplicable guidance at desperate times, and miracles that have saved me when crazy risk-taking could have taken me out.

I'm also aware of the gifts bestowed on me along my path at stages when I've tackled adversity and faced seemingly insurmountable challenges. I appreciate that at pivotal times I've received rewards and encouragement for my efforts.

My trip to New York was one of those times.

25

Magic Carpet Ride

I believe in magic and miracles, and I'm thankful for my mysterious benefactors. This story comes from a time when I had well and truly come out of the fog.

It was the year 2010, seven years after our beloved Joe died suddenly in an accident, and for the first time since then I was about to go overseas for two and a half weeks on my own. My daughter and I had been like two peas in a pod, recovering together from the devastating loss of her dad and my soulmate.

I was excited and terrified to be going to New York City to attend and present at the Shedding Light on Adoption conference. It was a huge step outside of my comfort zone, and I nearly backed out on several occasions. A friend was going to stay at my house and take care of my daughter, the house and our pets, and I was about to unburden my responsibilities and let go of the extremely difficult last seven years since Joe's death.

Part of my preparation was a visit with my long-time trusted psychic, who told me that Joe would be with me on the trip and that he was going to pull a few strings for me. It was a surprise reassurance that Joe was looking out for me, but I soon forgot all about my reading in the crazy chaos leading up to my departure.

I was edgy and anxious the whole way to the airport, and as usual I was running late. As I stood in the mile-long line at security, almost bursting at the seams with angst because boarding was imminent, I heard my name being called over the loudspeaker: 'Rabekah Scott-Heart, please make your way to the boarding gate.' I panicked. I thought they must be boarding already.

I politely jumped queue and raced with all my clobber at breakneck speed, arriving at the gate fully frazzled, only to see everyone standing around and sitting calmly, still waiting to board.

I went up to the desk and the flight attendant asked me for my boarding pass. 'You've been upgraded to first class and here's your new boarding pass,' she said.

I was speechless. It was like a dream. And the dream didn't end there.

From that moment, I had the most magic ride I have ever experienced in my life. Every planned and unplanned day of my trip was a diamond day. No stress, no struggle, nothing but joyous surprises, beautiful people, unexpected invitations, dancing, and dates with men.

And when I left New York to fly home, I was upgraded again! A help-yourself bar with endless Moet champagne, a continuous menu, a flat bed, pyjamas and a beautiful bathroom are some of the luxuries that made those two flights totally painless. It was truly miraculous. Joe really was pulling those strings for me.

Back to the initial flight from Brisbane to Los Angeles. I was feeling like a first-class queen, having taken my dinner up to the bar area, where I could sit on a stool and boggle at the booze. While I was there, an older Jewish American man came up to me and introduced himself. His name was Joel. He asked me where I was from and when I told him the Sunshine Coast Hinterland, he said that he had just been there looking at real estate.

To my surprise, I heard myself say, 'Don't buy there, go to Byron Bay.'

He feigned falling onto the bar as he responded, 'That's exactly what I did do.'

Then he revealed that he had seen a psychic in New York who told him that he was going to meet a woman from Queensland whom he would connect with. He said that it was divine intervention that we were on the same flight because he'd had to reschedule his flight from the previous day.

Joel and I talked more on the flight to Los Angeles, and we got along very well. We disembarked together and headed towards our departure gates for the next leg. Then Joel said he would like to continue our conversation, and he offered to pay for me to join him on his flight to New York. Okay, sounds good. Sure.

I had organised to stay in a low-cost women's hostel in New York, but I'd had great difficulty communicating with the hostel reception before I left Australia and didn't feel comfortable with my arrangements. On the Virgin America flight to New York I told Joel about my misgivings.

'You're welcome to stay at my place,' he said. 'I have plenty of room. My driver will pick us up from the airport and drive us directly to my home in Connecticut.'

Sounds great, I thought again. I should mention here that I trust my gut when I meet people, and in my gut I felt that Joel was trustworthy.

We drove along a tree-lined driveway and arrived at Joel's stunning mansion, which was surrounded by beautiful fall-coloured forest. Inside his split-level stone-and-wood home, with walls of glass that looked out over nature, were his eclectic art collection, sculptures on plinths, giant indoor plants, beautiful light, and a wonderful feeling of calm. Outside on the deck I saw two little chipmunks skittering about. This was the perfect place for me. *Thanks, Joel. Thanks, Joe.*

Over the next week Joel took me to dinners, on trips around New York, and to the Metropolitan Opera. I enjoyed freshly made delicious vegan meals prepared by a lovely young chef in Joel's support team. It was all a world away from my humble home and lifestyle.

Joel was the perfect gentleman and we had a great time. When it was time for me to go to my next accommodation near Central Park, Joel's driver took me there. I was rested, relaxed and ready for my next New York City adventure.

I presented at the Shedding Light on Adoption conference, where I met many amazing adoptees, and attended a heartfelt and moving support-group meeting in New Jersey. And the fun didn't stop there. I had so many magic encounters, almost enough to fill a book. I can't remember one negative about that trip. It was truly something very special. I felt like an empress. I shone, and everyone I met reflected the light back to me.

26

Return

> 'I am the master of my fate,
> And the captain of my soul.'
>
> —'Invictus', William Henley

Are we the masters of our lives? Or are we products of our conditioning? Are we living an unconscious loop of repetitious thoughts and actions? Do we believe the negative self-talk that has permeated our psyche? How equipped are we to make good choices for ourselves that will lead to our health and happiness? Were we neglected as a child, and do we continue to neglect ourselves even now? Does our fear of abandonment make us people pleasers, determined not to upset anyone and be rejected? Are we denying our own needs to appease others? Are we living life authentically?

My old adoption narrative ran my life. I didn't make healthy choices in my life because my brain's operating system was based on fear. I was rerunning the unconscious story of abandonment. I was involuntarily continuing to re-wound myself. And what made it so hard for me to change was the insidious and overriding falsehoods perpetrated by the adoption system. This contributed to the fog that I have had to spend most of my life dispelling. The irony is that a scheme that purported to save children from the sinful stigma of illegitimacy is in fact the real reprobate.

I used to feel sad about my life and all the cruel things that had been done to me, and all the tragic losses I had suffered. I felt unhappy because I was not loved and did not have what I needed. *Poor me. Those bastards. If only. I've drawn the short straw.* And so on. I was giving away my life, and the potential for my life, to some 'other' to determine the quality of my life. This was tantamount to offering up my most precious thing in this world (my life) to and for someone or something to make me wither or blossom. External influences defined who I was and whether I experienced love, joy, peace, happiness, depression, anger, hopelessness, or any other emotion. I was living from the outside in rather than from the inside out. I was being reactive instead of proactive.

Although this was understandable based on my early life, I realised that remaining in victim thinking was not serving me. I now know that I am the conductor of my own mind and emotions, and the designer of my reality. It was up to me to determinedly push against my default programming, and create new habits and pathways that brought my heart desires into reality. We are sovereign souls. Let our hearts lead the way.

Based on my life experience and learning, following is the treasure I found at the end of a rocky but ultimately rewarding road.

What I've learned

I've learned that taking a baby from mother at birth creates a deep fracture in the body, mind and soul, and that it can take a lifetime to recover and rebuild.

I've learned that although I was a victim in my early life, I am now one hundred percent responsible for the quality of my life, thoughts and happiness.

I've learned that understanding and forgiveness is for me—not for them; that to lead a positive and contented life it's important to try to forgive and let go of the perpetrators of pain. That doesn't mean that we condone their actions, we just need to release our victim thoughts and feelings.

We attract more of what we think. Attitude is everything. We can generate a bitter poor-me life, a beautiful and wondrous life, a life of abundance or lack, a life that is fun, or ho-hum, it's up to us. As Leon Brown says, 'Do not allow negative experiences to make you bitter, they should make you wiser, and with that wisdom you shall find joy.'

It's important to focus on what we want rather than what we didn't get and don't have. When we sow seeds of self love and believe that we deserve what we desire ... those longings will blossom in our lives. This is our life to choose and shape. What do we want more of? Because what we focus on comes to fruition. I've experienced this timeless magic.

I've learned that beyond the masks and roles that a human being wears and inhabits, there is a core essence, a unique spark of the all-encompassing light. We are part of the divine where we are not separate alone or suffering, where we are all connected in love.

I've learned how important it is to know that we matter! To let go of self-criticism and unworthiness. To fundamentally and wholly accept ourselves. To value and express our unique selves.

Like everyone else in this world, we've had negative experiences and have made mistakes. Despite any perceived fuck-ups, we deserve to be loved, to be happy, to have joy, to be respected and supported. It's time to be confident and strong in who we are, warts and all. Invest our love in people who treasure and reciprocate our love.

I've learned that love is a verb. How do we act from love? What would love do? How would love talk? Treating ourselves lovingly is number one priority. When we stop dwelling in the energy of anger, self-devaluation or lack, everything changes for the better. Separation trauma is something that happened to us when we were whole and healthy and connected to our essence. We are not at fault for the circumstances of our birth. Forced adoption was a flawed system; we are not flawed.

I've learned to challenge my core beliefs, to be mindful of my thoughts, and identify which ones are true, take me up or take me down. Unruly repetitive negative thinking keeps us diminished. Think well. Think big, not small. Live a life of largesse. Why not? It's not for everyone, but personally I love largesse.

'Start living large and in charge,' says Jen Sincero. I've often thought that the best thing about achieving success and having money is that you can give it away to help other beings out of suffering. Even without money we can uplift others, and ourselves, with art, inspiring books, the natural world and positive people.

I've learned that every human who comes to this earth deserves to be nurtured in love, validated, supported, positively regarded, and encouraged to be the best version of themselves. Whether or not we were given these priceless pearls, we can begin to practise giving them to ourselves through our self-dialogue, self-commitment, and action that takes us forward.

Original disconnection has paradoxically taught me that connection is everything and everything is connected. The spiritual lesson contained in my adoption story is that we are all interconnected. Due to and despite being amputated from my mother at birth, my life learning and definitive message is that human beings need connection just as much as the air we breathe. Life isn't worth living without it. As a child I connected to animals, which were my comfort and loving sustenance. But reconnecting with myself has been my greatest challenge and reward.

When we honour and nurture our connection to our essential self, we blossom.

We as a society need to value and support family connection, beginning with birth and the primal maternal bond, because how we are born matters. The strength of a child's physical foundation is built on their entry to the world. From womb to world needs to be a gentle transition sustained in love, giving the child the best chance of living their best life. When an infant is held and guided from birth, that child knows and grows their internal connection to their own soul.

Coming from a past dominated by trauma and anxiety, I've learned to no longer buy into fear. I heard someone say that there are two paths in life, faith or fear. I choose faith. When we have faith in ourselves, in our deep knowing, and in the love that surrounds us and is within us, we can feel safe and relaxed in our centre of peace.

Meditation, yoga, time in nature are a few ways to support this focus. Like a firmly planted tree, living life from a solid centre fortifies our ability to weather storms.

I've come to realise that we are resilient and resourceful, having been through some very difficult circumstances. Clarissa Pinkola Estes, author of *Women Who Run with the Wolves*, believes that 'those who have been "abandoned" and face it and work it through become the strongest people on the face of the earth'.

27

Community

> 'A group in which free conversation can take place. Community is where I can share my innermost thoughts, bring out the depths of my own feelings, and know they will be understood ... Communication makes community and is the possibility of human beings living together for their mutual psychological, physical and spiritual nourishment.'
>
> —Rollo May

After seven years and many thousands of dollars spent on therapy, Sherrie Eldridge, author of *Twenty Life Transforming Choices Adoptees Need to Make*, doesn't believe 'there is any doctor or therapist who can understand an adoptee like a fellow adoptee unless that professional just happens to be an adoptee'. She believes that an hour with a fellow adoptee is better than weeks of therapy: 'There seems to be an "emotional language" only understood by another adoptee who has walked a mile in our shoes.'

When I was in New York I was invited to attend a support group in New Jersey, and I was moved to tears by the strength of their connectedness. They had been meeting for many years, sharing their stories and supporting each other. They had the kind of trust relationship that builds over a long time of getting to know someone. And most stunning was the sense I had that they all had each other's backs. They were an enviable example of community.

We all sat around a big wooden table set with delicious delights to nibble on while we relaxed and talked, all in our native language: the language of adoptees. Nothing compares to reuniting with people from the same planet. I loved every minute of being a part of their circle.

To my adoptee tribe who read this, I sincerely wish that through this book we will come together and strengthen our connection as a community of people who have a shared experience. I hope our adoption community will be a strong and audible voice, raised in equality among the myriad of voices within our society. I'd like to see more resources available for us to gather together and heal together, because I've found that telling our truth-full stories and being heard with openness and empathy is remarkably healing.

When members of the adoption community come together, we find that we have a unique understanding and fellowship, even a sense of kinship. We identify with the experience of having lost what most people take for granted, and for many people affected by adoption there is a great sense of relief in finding that we are not alone.

In support groups, I have heard adoptees say that at last they realise that they're not crazy after all, that there are other people who reflect and understand their thoughts and feelings. When adoptees 'come out' and talk about the realities of our experience, the spell of the adoption myth is broken, and we are free to express ourselves more authentically.

For adoptees still suffering from low self-esteem, shame, guilt, secrecy, depression, problems with intimacy, or any other form of separation pain related to adoption, I encourage you to open up slowly but surely and start the healing process. Sharing your story will lessen the load you carry.

Unburdening ourselves by talking about what's going on inside our mind and emotions has immeasurable therapeutic value. Support groups are powerful. They provide a safe environment to openly disclose aspects of being adopted that may have been kept private, perhaps for many years.

For progress in adoptees' personal lives, and for society to learn from past mistakes, the concealed and insidious legacies of adoption practice need to be exposed for healing to occur, just as a physical wound needs light and air to properly mend.

One frequent issue for adoptees that is talked about in support groups is the sense of disconnection and loneliness. Being part of a group where people understand and validate each other alleviates this feeling, and often the connection felt between people is deep and immediate. We are a remarkable community with much to offer each other, the wider society and the world.

The end and the beginning

Well, it's been a long road home. Is there any more compelling journey than the one home? For adoptees it is the toughest road to take because we were removed from our heartland in the first moments of our life. We had no memory of home, no photographs, no stories, and no roadmap.

If you are an adoptee who feels lost in the fog, disengaged, or betwixt and between, I hope that following my meandering road through these chapters has given you some ideas for finding and appreciating the treasure of yourself and the home of your heart. You are a wonderful, worthwhile person. You matter. You've had the strong spirit to survive an extremely disconnecting event when you were at your most vulnerable. You merit love, the very best of your love. You have much to offer the world and deserve all that the world has to offer.

I started my search when I was completely clueless that adoption was a fundamental issue in my life (as were the health professionals I sought help from). That's how thick the fog was back then. Yet I was driven by some part of me that wanted to heal my trauma-affected brain and body. I set off on an unnamed remote road with a fierce determination and steadfast faith, guided by signs and support that appeared inexplicably. As I learned more about the truth of my story and myself, the fog gradually thinned and I started to see more clearly. Becoming a more objective observer of the realities of my life has freed me from my previous all-consuming identification with my adoption story and associated PATSD.

My struggles with mental health, insecurity, self-doubt, low self-esteem, shame and addiction can all be traced to trauma. When I look back at the errors I've made, and wrong turns I've taken in my life, I can unequivocally say that fear was the underlying driver. I endured intense and persistent fear in my early life, and that fear became a mainstay: fear of rejection, fear of loss, fear of being mistreated, fear of expressing my needs and asserting boundaries, and fear of speaking up.

It's well known now that trauma in childhood can damage the brain with toxic stress and cause mental health problems throughout life, and if left untreated can put people at risk of physical disease. Gabor Maté states that most chronic illnesses originate from childhood trauma. The particular complex trauma suffered by adoptees, PATSD, is a hidden epidemic. People who suffer daily from anxiety, addiction, depression, loneliness, attachment difficulties, inability to sustain intimate relationships, and physical-health problems as a result of separation trauma and adoption loss continue to be unrecognised, invalidated and unsupported.

Our basic birthright was stolen from us. We lost the chance to be connected to and raised naturally by our mothers, to be part of our biological families, to know our identity, to retain our original birth certificates, and to know our ancestry.

Adopted people are among the most neglected people in society when it comes to acknowledgment of and assistance for post-trauma ill health. This injustice needs addressing.

Like many mothers back in the seventies and eighties, I was a big fan of the book *The Continuum Concept,* and the philosophy it espoused.

Written in the mid-seventies, author Jean Liedloff explains the importance of constant contact between baby and mother, right from birth. She writes that if this primal need isn't met it can lead to social and mental disorders. I agree.

So my message isn't new. But in these consumerist times, this universal fact needs to be reiterated. We need to get back to grass roots and revere natural birth. If we want to grow connected kids who develop well into adulthood, and who in turn have a healthy connection to their social world and their broader environment, we must not separate them from their mothers at birth. Children who are not preoccupied by fight-flight-or-freeze reactions to trauma, and other related psychological and emotional issues, stand a greater chance of reaching their best potential.

If I had just one wish for my fellow adoptees, it would be to know your worth. That you matter. So many of my adoptee friends and acquaintances over the years have had trouble with this. At worst, they feel so unworthy and self-destructive that they hammer themselves with drugs and alcohol, or act out in other harmful ways. Or they are plagued by self-doubt and anxiety. Or they fluctuate between feeling okay and feeling like they're forever flawed. It's my wish for them to understand that they're reacting to past trauma and that *they* are completely loveable and deserve only love, not self-punishment. I like what Anne Heffron has said about adoptees: *'In my eyes adoptees are great-full—full of great because we faced down obliteration of the self when other people our age were getting held and named.'*

For a big part of my life I felt that I wasn't good enough, that I was insignificant and less than, which made me vulnerable prey and kept me in a re-wounding cycle. This hidden hell was isolating. I couldn't ask for help because I hadn't learned how to express my feelings and needs and be responded to. Until then I went through many episodes of great difficulty alone, because I didn't feel deserving of support, care, attention or love.

The truth is, it was all lies.

I remember seeing a T-shirt with the slogan: *If you're not living on the edge, you're taking up too much room.* It made me proud to be a fringe dweller. Seemed like an ethical option. It's been an interesting and exciting place to hang out, but it does feel great to jump down to Earth from that stratospheric fringe and be known, to myself and to others.

I've often thought of the movie *Sliding Doors* whenever I've considered how my other life might have played out had I not been (r)ejected and relocated at birth. Sometimes it seems like the life I've lived has been a stunted struggle to find the roots of that other life, that other me. However, I keep returning to who I am now and making the most of the rest of my life. Every moment is an opportunity to share, grow and enjoy life, a chance to love. Making meaning from experience is treasure we can all share.

So here I am in my sixtieth year, having spent most of my life recovering from the consequences of my shattered beginning, and I finally feel like me. A solid and real, fully fleshed-out human, living (not lost) on planet Earth.

The cascading consequences of forced adoption are inestimable. Adoptees need a voice (megaphone, please). We need to be heard.

It is especially important today with the burgeoning and cruel commoditisation of babies. Through our lived experience, adoptees can contribute our unique understanding to ethically inform this growing industry.

It's time for my adoptee community to be recognised for the inequalities we continue to bear, for the pain of disconnection, and for the cost to our personal lives.

When babies are nurtured and allowed to grow as wholehearted, connected children, they have the right foundation to grow into hale and hearty adults.

> 'There are only two lasting bequests we can hope to give our children; one is roots and the other is wings.'
>
> —Henry Beecher

Finally, some winged words from the most deeply rooted, fully embodied force of nature I've ever known:

'... Just fly!'

—Joe Scott

www.ingramcontent.com/pod-product-compliance
Lightning Source LLC
Chambersburg PA
CBHW030254010526
44107CB00053B/1708